I Could Write A Book:

So I thought I'd try online dating LOL

By Karen M. Blaisdell

I Could Write A Book:
So I thought I'd try online dating LOL
First edition, Paperback – published 2012

ISBN-13: 978-0615586748 (KMB)
ISBN-10: 0615586740

This book is a work of non-fiction. All the names of those depicted have been changed to protect their identity. Any resemblance to a particular person or dating story may not be construed to, in fact be a particular person or dating story based on content alone.

Illustration by Jacob DeRemer

Dedications

To all of the serious searchers, hopeless romantics and optimists, may you find your sunset.

To all of the game players, cheaters, users and the like...thanks for the material.

To "V", you know who you are. Without you I'd of surely sunk. To you I leave a heartfelt and lifelong thank you.

Table of Contents (Summary)

Table of Contents-Cont'd.

Disclaimer

I've decided to replace the Preface of my book with this disclaimer in an attempt to avoid any unwarranted remarks for my musings. Please be sure to read it in its *entirety*, as I am *hardly* presumptuous enough to assume anything about your experiences.

What you are about to read, might not have happened to you in this particular way or at *all* for that matter. This is indeed *my* story with bits and pieces of experiences from other people whose paths I've crossed throughout this process. Occasionally, it was a pleasure to meet them, but there were a *lot* of displeasures while online dating as well.

I do not have a PhD or *any* degree for that matter; it's a work in progress. However, what I *do* have is a plethora of participation in the 21ˢᵗ century's online dating drama and the passion to write about it. This book is predominantly written from the female perspective. Let's face it, without a penis, it's not plausible to write in the males; but there are *definitely* he's that can be replaced with she's...so don't despair.

Our gender differences are *vast*, but I have found that all of the experiences people have with online dating—oddly enough— mirror each other's more often than not. I am sure there have been many or at the very least *some* who have sustained a suitable experience via online. Nevertheless, I have also learned through my dating travels that there are many more that have *no*t. If there is a trend with online dating, I would argue it to be the disappointment in this all too easy avenue to ever-lasting love. Learn to laugh, it will be your saving grace and is a requirement to survive online dating.

This book is *my* attempt at laughing at the past three years of my life...in the hopes of giving the past three years of my life purpose. I would like to think that I've accomplished *something* for my blood, sweat and carpal tunnel.

Try not to be *too* cynical by the offerings in this book. I fully realize that *there are exceptions to every rule*. Sometimes, I wonder what it would feel like to *be* the exception, but that's neither here nor there. I've seen it work...though rare. If at *any* point you feel offended or feel the need to disagree with what's written, please turn back to this page and re-read this disclaimer—in particular—*there are exceptions to every rule*. I cannot say it enough and despise redundancies, so I refuse to repeat it through each chapter. This is my effort to reduce the chances that I've offended someone in our overly sensitive, politically-correct society. Who knows, maybe the omission of repetition will save a page...and a tree.

I have yet to decide, which dusty shelf this book *may* or may *not* have the honor of sitting on. Is it a self-help, how to or a biography of sorts? I would imagine you will pull from it whatever it is you are seeking, so I won't attempt to dictate what it will be for *you*. It's quite possible; I'm just tired of trying to figure it out myself as well. However, it is my *sincere* hope that what it *will* be is an opportunity for you to see yourself or maybe your last daunting date, allowing you to relate and with *any* luck...laugh a little.

"Half of the journey is imagining the possibilities, the other half is the destination once those possibilities are realized; don't miss out on the journey...it's the best part."

Introduction

"Perhaps an epic fail in future plans, is really the universe's way of keeping you on the path to something grander that otherwise, you'd of missed."

The end to my fifteen-year marriage, begged the question, "Is this the beginning or is it the end"...to my life that is. For me, it was the beginning, but I suppose the answer to that question is different for everyone.

The precursor to the "beginning" or to the "end," I believe, is dictated by how it ended. Were you, the divorcer or the divorced, the committed or the commitment phobe, the anguished or the antagonist? It also depends on our perception and general outlook on life as a whole. Are you optimistic or pessimistic, a goal seeker or a pacifist? Do you believe life is a journey of choices with rewards and consequences or a divinely created destiny that plays out just as it should?

This book is my spin on 21st century dating. It is written from my experiences and the experiences of those I've met throughout this process. I've learned and listened enough to know, that it resembles the story of many seekers, both men and women alike. It is written, not just as my biographical journey through this new process for finding love; but for those hopeless romantics who have endlessly searched for "The One," that for one reason or another have evaded them. With laughter, some cynicism and a bit of hope, I have managed to master the craziness that was, is and will forever remain online dating.

There is a learning curve with this style of dating and it seemed never ending. At every turn, there was something else to factor into finding someone, on some occasions making the process rather maddening. The most intriguing thing I'd learned, however, is that the dating world is *not* defined by gender or age. It didn't seem to matter how I got here, or how long I'd be staying. It mattered even less, what I'd been through or even what I was looking for. Indeed, the online dating world—it appeared—was and is universal in its heart-wrenching, confusing and sometimes comical twists and turns along the way to never-ending happiness...if it *does* exist.

I suppose like anything else, "comical" would depend on what one considers funny. I found laughter to be my saving grace when I was my *most* frustrated and my *most* frustrated, had without a doubt been displayed time and time again over these past three years. Try though I may, punching pillows and complaining to my friends wasn't eliminating my post bad date frustration fast enough, so I laughed and wrote instead. Unfortunately, I found that more often than not my own mistakes and naiveté *were* the punch lines.

It didn't surprise me that the younger generation seemed much less perplexed by the utter disheveled mess, which had become dating these days. They were, however, just as dis-enchanted by the disingenuous online dating world of the 21st century, as the seasoned-singletons were. These seasoned-singletons had the disadvantage of remembering the old days when boy meets girl, boy likes girl, boy asks girl out were the only precursors to a potential relationship. For us, dating in the 21st century left a world to be reckoned with, as we em-barked on a journey to find just *one* who remembered and valued it too.

I'm thinking it was probably a huge advantage that our younger counterparts didn't have the same recollection of dating etiquette that we did. They had nothing to compare the craziness of online dating to; it's all they've known. How-ever, it did make me wonder what might be worse, never knowing the greatness of what dating used to mean or yearn-ing for something that quite possibly no longer exists.

When I started the thought process of writing this book, I found myself really embarrassed by the outcome to my online dating experiences. After three years of picking through the dating garden, all I had to show for it was blisters and a bag full of weeds. After *three years*, that felt long when I was lonely and short when I was preoccupied, I was *still* no closer to finding "The One." Impossible, I thought to myself. Is it, me? In retrospect, it absolutely was not...well not completely. This isn't a contradiction. I am merely admitting that although I would like to proclaim myself to be the picture of perfection, I'm actually *not* perfect. I know, *shocking*. At least my father would argue that I am...thanks dad.

The truth is, in the end, I am a mere mortal. This means that I come with many imperfections, idiosyncrasies and yes, even faults. With those human traits as a back-drop, it can only mean that I have most certainly been the subject of a dating horror story or two. It's not that I was one of the off-colored datables, for whom you will have a detailed list later in this book..."AD" days aside of course; but more because I didn't know who I was or what I wanted, and I had *no* business looking until I did.

Although this identity crisis is not *thee* biggest problem with online dating, it ranks pretty high up on the reason list for my personal failure to find my "Mr. Right." There were *too* many "I don't know what I want or who I am" singles, signing up and logging in. After what I've done and what I've bared witness to, I'd have to say that most people post-split *don't* know who they are or what they want. I believe, this is why our first steps back into the dating world, inevitably take us right to the internet. Why? Because it's easy and everything in our lives after a break-up feels *uneasy*, so *easy* is appealing. Everything in my life that I knew and had grown comfortable with had changed. However, it didn't change the important fact that defining myself before I started to look for someone, before *anyone* starts looking—really—is a necessary, but much too often missed step that has disastrous consequences.

When all was said and done—I'm *so* over online dating—I realized that although while writing this book, I am still a seeker; I did find something of value...research. I can assure you that research certainly wasn't my goal, at least not in the beginning; but I was grateful to have *something* to show for the three-hundred dates, I'd subjected myself to. I'm sure "subjected" seems like a very strong word to define a date, but it is a *more* than suitable description of my journey through "Mr. Wrongs."

I would like to elaborate on "three-hundred dates." I considered a cup of coffee with a ten-minute conversation a date. Sadly, there were many more of *those* than anything that even remotely resembled what I would have considered a *real* date. In fact, I found myself feeling quite envious, a bit irritated and *definitely* bitter at the Match.com commercials. These depictions of an upscale restaurant where the matches sat laughing, and an obvious connection had been made, were disheartening at best. All *I* ever seemed to get was the local pub, sexual innuendos and the bill.

I can't help but wonder how many dates it took to get to this dating nirvana. Was it their first, second, twentieth? Were they actors or *actual* couples? Do *actual* online couples exist? What happened when the cameras turned off? Did he ask her to spend the night? Start sexting her? Did he *ever* bother to respond to another call, email or text again?

And so here I am at the end of my online journey, ready to share my *"research"* with the world. Perhaps you will find yourself in the pages that follow, or maybe you will read this before taking the primitive plunge into the dating pool. I can assure you, it is *anything* but evolved. In fact, text messages, emails and the like have led to the digression in the evolution of dating *so* much so, that it feels more like I've been clubbed over the head by technology and drug back to the dating cave, where I have to bang on rocks in Morse code as my source of communication...*if* I feel like responding that is.

Indeed, this is a biography of sorts, but it isn't my story alone. It's the story of many who yearn to find that someone special. And though I haven't found my "Mr. Right" *yet*, I am happy to announce that I did end up finding myself while trying to survive the 21st century's rendition of dating.

As you turn the pages, of "I Could Write a Book" I hope you find laughter and in the end...maybe "The One." At the very least, however, I'm hoping as I did, you will end up finding yourself. It's something you *need* to find before you can live "happily ever after." There is no "*and they*" in "they lived happily ever after" without *you*.

So I ask you, "Is this the beginning...or is it the end" ...to *your* life that is? That's a question you'll have to answer for yourself, but for now, it's the beginning of this book.

Don't waste the space: Leave your heartache from your last relationship on this page...then turn it!

Chapter 1

2007 "AD"
The aftermath

"Sometimes you have to clean the cobwebs from the corners of your life...before you can sit back and bask in the glory of a job well done."

Don't waste the space: Leave an embarrassing story about yourself during your transition from couple to single...for your eyes only!

This *isn't* a chapter about Christ, although I've certainly used his name enough in the last three years. This was my precursor into the dating world. It was my first steps into the light of a different life, as I revealed myself to the new possibilities. I had no idea; it was anything *but* me...thank God. The definition of "AD" is "After Division" and was jokingly applied to me, *by* me, post-split from my long-term marriage. Actually, I would call it a dictatorship more than a marriage, but that's a separate chapter *all* on its own...hell, *that's* another book. At first, I thought the title was cute, before I realized what it encompassed. What does it mean? Simply put, it means mindlessly reckless behavior that could only appropriately be titled "Rebel without a cause."

At the moment of separation, I seemed to rebel against anything that even *remotely* encompassed adulthood, as I reverted back to my younger years. Partying, wasting money and embracing promiscuity were my new commandments. The recollection of it regularly makes me makes me blush at the thought now. In the twilight zone that *was* a separation for me, I've learned that I *wasn't* alone. My "AD" transition indeed was shared by many marriage misfits who aimlessly wandered about in search for some semblance of a self, once detached from everything they knew. In fact, I was *far* from the exception...I *was* the rule. From laundry and PTA to lipstick, pubs and clubs, life had certainly changed.

There is, without a doubt, a metamorphosis that ensues post-split, superseding gender or even sensibility. It is an odd phenomenon and only whispered among the spectators...so as not to provoke the obviously insane individual transitioning. Mine was an awkward stage, as I roamed through the hurt haze, carrying my bruised relationship baggage and brainlessly bumped into people.

For those who had bi-passed, somehow escaped or never had to contend with this type of transition, well, they became very easy targets for an "AD" ambush. These unknowing and innocent victims were sure to suffer from my temporary deterioration in behaving even *remotely* human. I casually and carelessly went from one to the next; unaware of the damage I was leaving in my wake. I suppose these were necessary steps since I had lost my identity post divorce. Each irresponsible act was, somehow, a vital component of putting me back together again; as I evolved from who I was, into who I would become. It was, however, a bumpy road for those in my path and *not* one of my prouder moments in life. Most close acquaintances saw the change in me, although many were unable to put their finger on what was happening? Of course, if they were recovering AD'aholics, they merely turned their heads to avoid watching the train wreck.

It's been my experience, that nothing can stop the transitioner from the error of their ways; any more than you can stop a horse from racing towards the finish line. I've attempted to save a few friends from the transition, which proved to be an impossible task; *just* as impossible as it was when *they* tried to save me.

Sadly, not all "AD" budding butterflies complete their metamorphosis. Indeed, some remain stuck with that misbehaving mentality. Luckily, for singles everywhere, those are usually easy to spot. Once my "AD" fog had lifted, I had *no* problems deciphering who they were.

"Take a year to heal," was the often doled advice from those individuals lucky enough to sustain the day to day monotony of marriage or a union of sorts. It was solid advice for sure, but my wings had *hardly* grown. That advice would have been better aimed at those who were in the path of my "AD" antics. At that time in my life, any normal advice passed through my ears and landed on my brain like a foreign language, which I had *no* intention of learning how to speak.

Though it is certainly true that I needed time to heal, I could only see my situation as freedom. It was easy or perhaps just convenient, to deny my feelings of absolute failure and disappointment, in my *not* so happily ever after ending to my "old" life. Truth be told, the "AD" singleton is *going* to recklessly transition. That *is* their healing process. I suggest that perhaps that advice would be better suited, for the singles in their path. The distance of a year is great advice that *someone* should listen to, mine as well say it to someone who can hear it.

I don't know if I was grasping for my youth and the years I felt I had lost when I was with my insignificant other, which precipitated this behavior. God *knows* I did everything, but build a time machine. Maybe it was the process of recreating myself minus the rituals of a relationship, because what *was* I if I wasn't washing his underwear and making his dinner. Perhaps it was the utter bliss of freedom. After all, being free again was like eating hot fudge sundaes every day *without* gaining an ounce...or so I thought.

Little did I know that my destructive behavior was making my problems *fatter* by the minute? It indeed haunted me with remorse and outright shock at some of the decisions I had made, and quite carelessly. More often than not, these decisions would put me in dicey positions, which created over time, a learned behavior of self-destruction and a lack of self-worth. Of course it took me some time to realize the damage I was causing.

What I know now, in no uncertain terms, is that there was *no* "longevity" during my "AD" days, though I proclaimed that to be my goal. In fact, it was completely omitted from the script of my life, as a whole. Though I looked relentlessly for someone to occupy my time, I couldn't allow them to stay there for *too* long, branding them throw-aways, as I left casualties of *my* war through every city in Eastern Michigan.

You may be asking yourself how or why I've given a name to the "AD" Singleton. First and more importantly, because people who are seriously searching *need* to know that they *are* out there. There needs to be an understanding about the mindset of the people coming out of relationships. Since I had put in my time as one, I figured it was fitting for me to name it. Of course, it also helps that it's my book. Couple those reasons with the fact that I tried to date some, had friends transitioning and shamefully spent a night with a few, and it only fueled the need for a name. With all of that being said, I feel confident in my description of this particular persona.

Though there was no medal-of-honor or degree once I graduated...or should I say grew wings; it *certainly* was an accomplishment to heal enough to crack the cocoon and become a fully functional butterfly. It's difficult for me to remember *everything* that transpired that year. Of course, it just might be my subconscious refusal, to retrospect through the shameful hue of havoc that *was* my life for that year. It is pretty bad when you blush, and you're alone.

I will admit that on occasion I do reminisce and indeed even miss the "*me*" through that transition. Not so much for my behavior during that time, but for how I felt about myself. That person—who is now nothing more than a stranger to me—was fun and funny, adventurous and active, confident and carefree. It's not that I don't still possess *some* of those character traits, but their makeup is different. Now I have to work a little harder to feel that way, on a day to day basis. Oddly enough, the freedom to date gave me the confidence to see myself in that light, but the freedom to date *also* took it away.

My most missed attribute, however, was my attitude and belief that I was completely indestructible. Though I know now that I really *wasn't*, at the time I truly felt untouchable. For one solid year, I was unwittingly, yet oddly happily subscribed, to a code of unethical, morally misconstrued and self-absorbed unwritten laws. It didn't matter if they were right or wrong, they were mine for the taking...or was that breaking? Breaking just seems more on target.

I could go on and further break down the chaos of this colossal conundrum in my life. However, I'm guessing that partying, wasting money and promiscuity are cue enough for *anyone* to "get" the picture. I'd prefer to avoid throwing myself under the "bimbo" bus repetitively, if possible. Chances are if you've experienced a split, especially from a long term anything, you have also grasped at the "stages" straws. It seemed I had on more than *one* occasion during my healing process. It was no big surprise that I tended to pick the shortest one, more often than not. Of course, these "stages" made the short straw *just* fine, at that time. I can assure you, in retrospect, if I had it to do over again, I *wouldn't* have played the game to begin with. In the end, I think I can assume you understand what I'm saying here, *without* the added need for a detailed description of my own personal train wreck. Let's face it, my hints are pretty transparent.

If, by chance, you picked this book up in the hopes of getting a glimpse into the online dating dish, before breaking out your utensils and taking a bite. Well, there's *more* than a side dish here to help you with your decision on delicacies. So tuck in that napkin and open your menu to dating in the 21st century...or is it dissing? I think *dissing* just seems more apropos.

Don't waste the space: Leave a short note about someone you noticed in transition...they'll be so much easier for you to spot now!

Chapter 2

If I Build It...He Will Come

"If hope has wings, let them unfurl and carry me on the breeze of belief, to soar above the chaos of the world and take refuge under the breast of love."

Don't waste the space: Leave your hopes and dreams of your perfect match...you'll laugh at it later!

Online dating isn't the wave of the future; rather, it's quickly becoming the demise of tangible dating. We have convinced ourselves, it's the easiest way to meet someone, while we endure our hectic lives. Unfortunately, this thought process is really just a lie. Just like anything in life, if we *continuously* repeat something to ourselves, we are bound to convince ourselves that it's truth. Besides, if we don't have the time to put into meeting someone in the *real* world, then how do we have time to denote to a relationship if we do find one?

It only stands to reason, that in this quick gratification society, we would turn to the internet in the hopes that we'll conveniently find ourselves a significant other. It is the perfect, impersonal "I can delete you on a whim" alternative to *actual* human contact. With little time invested, we have little to lose. Online dating is simply *too* easy. It allows people to become whomever it is they wish to be, with some semblance of anonymity. If in the end, we are only willing to give a *little* of ourselves, we shouldn't be so shocked when what we *get*, is only a little in return.

At first glance, it's overwhelming; as I happily clicked through page after page of my future possibilities, all stacked in neat columns and rows. They felt reminiscent to the penny candy bins I ravaged as a kid and *almost* as exciting. There was always a teaser, to get you to taste the forbidden fruit that lied *just* beyond the membership key too. You were only allowed so many browses and *no* contact, before you were stopped *dead* in your tracks, with an offer to entice you to to come inside and play.

Jumping in with both feet, I eagerly built my profile and pulled my credit card from my wallet. I remember the feeling the first time I pressed the "buy it now" key, thinking my prince charming would be carefully placed in my cart. What a unique concept, that I could plug in my deepest desires, push the enter key, and he would *magically* appear. Or *was* it? The intrigue and value of boy meets girl was instantly usurped by a resume format, which left *little* to the imagination. The daydreams of discovering who he may be were coldly brushed aside, as I looked for signs of my possible future on profiles that *all* looked the same.

Most of us women start out our lives with fairytales of happily-ever-after...including me. It's *really* no big surprise that I ended up disappointed. To my recollection, the story *didn't* end with Prince Charming having a one-night stand with Cinderella or the Prince disliking the shorter locks of Repunzel. No one *ever* read me the story of him waking Snow White with a kiss, only to continue kissing other women, for fear he *might* be missing the next-best thing. This is not to suggest that online dating *never* works. I'm sure my friend Kim's friend Donna, who knew a girl Gina that dated John, really *did* know Stefanie, who found the love of her life on Match.com. I would simply argue that Stefanie, who knew John, that dated Gina, who knew a girl Donna, that was friends with Kim, is more the *exception* than the rule.

In the beginning, I was filled with optimism and why *shouldn't* I be, with fifty perfect matches filtered into my inbox. I'd like to know who came up with this *all* powerful "Oz" of relationship software that decided "Bigone4u" was the man of my dreams, anyway. So as a newbie on the dating www, I built my profile with words like optimistic, hopeful, romantic and passionate, and I *searched*, and I *waited*, and I *searched*, and I *dated*, and eventually I became persistently pessimistic, depressed, frigid and pissed off. Imagine how *that* profile would be received...if I had bothered to change it. Then again, most don't bother to change much of anything.

Of course, when I was a newbie, I assumed all profiles were written with the honesty and integrity that I had used when writing my own. In retrospect, I suppose they were written with as much honesty as one can muster about themselves, minus the obvious asshole that will *never* grow wings. They *are* out there...buyers beware. Is it misleading that we *only* write the good stuff? How many would read past "Looking for Mr. Right," if it was immediately followed with "Occasionally bitter and untrusting over my horrendous split, with intermittent bouts of depression because I'm lonely?" What are the chances the profile *I* was perusing had been embellished or that "Mr. Right" had stretched the truth, while building *his* profile? Very little...I'm sure. In case you didn't catch it that was sarcasm.

After years of over indulging myself in optimism, I have come to the conclusion that I can wrap any profile I want in a silver lining; but in the center of it all, there was *still* a looming dark cloud. It took a bit of time, but eventually I recognized the key words and phrases that although were stated one way, really meant something *completely* different. Of course, I still chose to ignore the red flags and push forward into yet *another* disheartening date in my pursuit for the fairytale.

I thought it would behoove me to give my readers something they could ponder. Of course, it doesn't hurt to attempt to laugh at my own stupidity either. In my attempt to do that, I have taken the liberty of creating, from a past dating experience, an example of "Mr. Rights" profile. Enjoy this delusional display of self-righteous ridiculousness, before I enlighten you to the *less* than titillating truth.

♂♀

Searching for my soul mate, for however long God will let me have her. I am a hopeless romantic who's searched endlessly for my princess, but to no avail. It's important that I find the right one, rather than the one for right now. I prefer casual settings, where we can have a drink while we talk, and I love to people watch. The economy has taken its toll on us all, so I appreciate the little things and find no need to live an over-indulging lifestyle. My family is very important to me, and I spend ample time with them. I am looking for a woman who appreciates family as much as I do. I'm not much for talking on the phone; I believe that talking in person is much more personable, even if you can't talk as often as you'd like. Taking walks together are under-rated, but if you enjoy driving that's fine too. I have no children of my own but am open to the possibilities of children. I am eager to find the one to dote over and the one that will dote over me. Thanks for taking the time to read my profile.

♂♀

Had I understood the dating profile language from the beginning, I can assure you I could have weeded him out faster. Can a date or "get to know you" discussion, *be* any faster than ten minutes? Now enlightened with the online dating lingo, please allow me to familiarize you with his actual and less than eloquent, between the lines' meaning.

♂♀

Searching for a sucker for a one-night stand. I've never been married because I have commitment and monogamy issues. I drink every weekend and can often be found at the local watering hole, where I ogle the scantily dressed babes. I work very hard at my part-time job, which usually leaves me too exhausted to phone you when I get home. I spend what little money I do make on the lottery, after I give my mother her half, as my rent for living in her basement. You must live close or have a car, as mine was impounded some time ago, from my last D.U.I. I don't have any children, so I'm selfish with my time, which means, I fully expect you to put my needs before your children. Thanks for taking the time to read my profile.

♂♀

In all honesty, the women aren't much better. However, in my own defense, though I may have embellished my happy-go-lucky attitude a bit, I was *never* quite this blatantly butchering with my description. I must say before proceeding, on behalf of *all* the women in the dating world truly seeking, it *pains* me to write this.

♂♀

Ready for "Mr. Right." A professional man is a must. One who is established, and goal oriented. I do have children and would only be involved with someone who enjoys them as much as I do. While I'm not looking for a man to replace their father, I am hoping to find someone who will accept them just the same. I believe life is too short, and we must live each day to the fullest, which is why you will always see me stopping to smell the roses. People often tell me I look younger than my age, and I say, age is just a number. I adore animals and would like someone who enjoys them as well. I believe communication is paramount in any relationship, and I pride myself on being a great communicator. I also believe that spending quality quiet time together, when time permits, is an important factor for us to get to know each other. I will be posting more pictures soon. Thanks for reading my profile.

♂♀

I'm sure that profile *seemed* normal enough. *Dare* I say it could qualify her as, quite a nice woman? I can assure you, that my friend who responded to that profile was more than a *little* traumatized from the outcome of the *actual* meeting. Perhaps a little decoding before his date could have spared him the nightmare. Don't be afraid to ask a friend who's been doing online dating for a while. In fact, I encour-

~ 21 ~

age you to...actually I *insist* As veterans, we have become *quite* proficient at picking up those all important, but often missed, "he's/she's crazy" code words from the *best* written profiles ...case in point.

♂♀

I am desperately seeking Mr. Perfect. He must make a boat load of money to support my four children, since I can't find my baby daddy...for any of them. I do, however, have a few paternity suits pending. I don't like to work, cook or clean, for that matter, but who cares; I make great arm candy. I'm not opposed to younger men, after all Cougars are the thing these days. If you leave a comment on the dog/cat pictures, I've posted, you'll earn extra brownie points. I fully expect you to be at my beckon call night or day and if you don't answer when I need you my neurosis will be displayed in all its glory which I cannot be responsible for, since I haven't had the time or money to refill my prescriptions. Please don't ask me for any other pictures, as I have lost my subscription to PhotoShop. Thanks for reading my profile.

♂♀

It amazes me, even now, that I could continue the façade of finding "Mr. Right" armed with this new knowledge. The task was difficult and became more impossible with each picked apart profile. In fact, finding him— if he *was* out there—would be the equivalent of finding the *one* ant that could move the rubber tree plant, *simply* because he had high hopes...but I pushed on.

It took some time, but my profile was finally perfected with words that were *sure* to grab the attention of the most eligible bachelor. It was now time to begin the grueling process of uploading photos. Of course, my profile wouldn't be complete without the *infamous* self-portrait picture. *That*, in and of itself, was a process.

As I surveyed all thirty self-esteem busting photos I *actually* took, with careful deliberation I selected the best photos, which meant, deleting twenty-nine and uploading...*one*. I then, denoted hours scrutinizing my existing photos, to be certain I included action shots to prove that I *wasn't* a spinster with a houseful of cats, and that I *indeed* had friends beyond my internet connections. Note to female friends: *Stop* posting pictures of your pets, you *aren't* doing us any favors. He's *not* looking to date your dog! A man may enjoy pets, but it usually isn't the precursor to his decision on whether or not to date you. However, if you *insist* on posting them anyway, don't make them your *main* profile picture for the *love* of God.

I can tell you that after oodles of online dating sites, I have *yet* to run across a profile of a man who seemed even semi-concerned about the quality of *his* photos. Indeed, photo etiquette is *definitely* a female trait. From beer bellies to bare chests, self-portrait of course, the male gender hasn't a clue on the female rules of said photo etiquette, leaving many to sit on the online dating shelf with the threat of expiration, due to bad goods.

Now that I was almost to the finish line, I sat back to bask in the glory of a job well done. I was certain that once my profile had been accepted by the *"Great* Online Oz," because he *is* the gatekeeper to the land of love, my finest qualities would *definitely* capture the interest of the man of my dreams. I just knew that he would be spell-bound by my words as he surveyed my lovely list of character traits and desires. Incidentally, my list of desires would have been *better* suited to be called demands.

So, I convinced myself that "If I built it, he would come." I had achieved the perfect profile, consisting of the perfect picture, for the perfect ending, to my imperfect life. I was, however, *completely* ill-prepared for the *not*-so-perfect outcome, to the *not*-so-perfect avenue that *is* online dating. As I sit here typing tales of my journey through a fruitless process, I can't help but introspect about why I might still be alone. I must admit, however, the further I get in this book, the more *obvious* the reasons appear. Its funny how things look so much different from where I'm sitting now, but then that's how it goes, there's always more clarity in retrospect.

Nevertheless, I realized that is what precipitated this book to begin with. I am *not* alone. My profile was mixed with many other profiles that may not have been perfect but all had *something* to offer. Okay, perhaps not *all* but at the very least...*some*. Besides, everyone is perfect for their perfect someone...right? Who determines what or who is perfect anyway? After all, perfection is in the eye of the perceiver...is it not? Many of us trusted in the "Great Online Oz" as we swooned over the "1 in 5 relationships start online" commercials, believing that "*we*" would be that "*one.*"...hell, I'm *still* waiting.

And so, I leave this chapter with yet *another* of my optimistically wrapped epiphanies. I believe that all is not lost and that there *is* a "someone" for everyone, in particular, me. Hey, I *said* I was optimistic. However, I think fairytales may have had it right all along, when they depicted Prince Charming riding up on his white steed. The 21st century may be loaded with technology, and we may *not* have need for horses anymore, but something tells me it would be *more* than a miracle to see him riding up on fiber-optic cables.

Chapter 3

Winks, Flirts and Friend Requests
Could there *be* a bigger hit to your self-esteem?

"Arrogance is very unbecoming. The moment you think you're all that, you just proved...you aren't."

Don't waste the space: Leave your first diss story...not the one you dissed either!

From Myspace to Match.com and from EHarmony to ItalianSingles, I've done it *all* in my quest for courting. Looking for love knows no bounds, so it only seemed fitting to break out the pocket book on as many sites as I could find. Let me tell you, that's *a lot* of sites and a *whole* lot of pocket book breaking. Apparently, I thought the odds would be in my favor the more sites I was on, but *that* is the mother of all misnomers. I wasn't the only one with this brilliant idea, rendering *most* if not *all* the profiles or possibilities the same. In all seriousness, it was like a recycle bin that *never* got emptied. God forbid a new member would come along in my area; it was akin to a feeding frenzy in a pond of starving piranha.

There was, however, one very distinct difference between said sites, my ability to virtually flirt. Incredible as it may seem, if I didn't have the gumption to send an email to an interest, there was always another avenue for first-time contact. Winks, flirts and friend requests were the supposed playful precursors to that first hello. Some sites took it shamefully further where I could *spank* the object of my online affection. Because *that's* appropriate to do before you even know the name of your admirer. Every time I think about the juvenile online flirt options, it reminds me of my 7th grade Science class; when I dropped a note on the desk of my bff asking her to find out if the dreamboat three seats down liked me. "Circle one yes/no"

Post-perusing hundreds of *seemed* to be possible potentials, I excitedly sent out my flirt of choice. Of course, I never expected it might not be reciprocated, or *acknowledged*, for that matter. Before I knew better or really even understood the logistics of the loathed diss, I waited for my response, sometimes for days. I waited *and* waited and *waited* annnnd waited. I mean, virtual flirting was humiliating enough; but now I had been technologically dissed, without *even* so much as a standard rejection letter...and I thought *those* were brutal. You would think with all of these virtual flirts and tech-savvy sites flying around, *someone* would have invented the "No thanks" or "Not Interested" button. It sure would have saved me a lot of time and perhaps spared me a few grey hairs to boot. And for those sites that actually *took* the time to create said button, why the *hell* doesn't anyone use it...sigh?

It's amazing how it had never dawned on me, that though they may be the object of *my* obsession, I may *not* be the object of theirs. Can you imagine? Apparently, I couldn't, as I repeatedly subjected myself to this form of technological torture. I chuckle to myself as I think back to my first experience, logging in and out like a crazed lunatic, desperate for a response. People wouldn't just completely ignore me would they? I mean surely he would have, at the *very* least, sent *something* back. Obviously, something was amiss perhaps an unpaid internet bill or maybe he was just busy writing me a lengthy response. However, once a week had passed with that pisser of a neon sign blinking "Online" in my face incessantly as if mocking me and he still hadn't responded, I finally *got* it.

I'm fairly certain; the shard of hurt and embarrassment that penetrated my heart and grappled with my soul of self-esteem is universal. It shattered me to morsels, and I began to sink to a new low with each passing flirt gone unnoticed. I mean, *come on*. I'm a catch...what an *idiot*. By now, my sarcasm should be obvious.

I doubt the diss would have felt that dreadful if I hadn't donned the dissing from time to time. For those of us who have traveled this self-righteous road, you know the drill. You get the flirt, then look at the profile and think to yourself, "He/she's *so* not in my league." Yes, I'm aware that's arrogant, but man up, if you've been online dating, you have thought it at *least* once. I've heard the stories so *spare* me the "holier than thou" sentiment. I'm hoping admittance will redeem me and cast out my unwanted crappy Karma. God knows I've collected enough of *that* during my "AD" days.

Without realizing it, in one keystroke or lack thereof, I myself, had sent someone else spiraling down self-loathing lane. I think for those of us who have endured and dished, we can *all* agree the "diss" is *definitely* one of the more painful parts of online dating. At the *very* least it's stinging to the self-esteem. Perhaps "Do unto others" would be good practice when virtually flirting. Can I still say that in this politically-correct society, it has a bit of religious undertone? Of course, I can. It's my book; I can say whatever I want.

As time passed, I surpassed irrational rookie and became a profile pro. The angst I felt over the non-response made me feel like a loser, but that feeling did eventually pass...thank *God*. Unfortunately, it had been replaced with a new feeling that wasn't much better. In fact, I'd argue it to be worse. "Go f&*k yourself" was my new sentiment of choice, which incidentally, was shouted at what had *now* become my significant other—the empty inbox—on a regular bases.

To add insult to injury, many of these sites offered me yet another avenue to torture my *already* flailing ego. That's right, as if being hug humiliated wasn't enough; they offered me the opportunity to purchase insurance...if you will. For a nominal fee—because the membership fee couldn't *possibly* cover this cost—I could buy the option to *see* if the email I had sent had been retrieved and read. Obviously, the site had malfunctioned...*again*. He must not have gotten my flirt, was my ridiculous reasoning, but nevertheless, it forced me to put away my smileys and contact him by email.

To this day, I cannot come up with a viable reason why they would offer this ego busting tool. I, for one, would prefer the old adage "Ignorance is bliss." I will now hang my head in yet *another* moment of shame as I admit that I had indeed purchased this self-inflicting torture. Apparently, my trusty cliché wasn't profound enough to stop me from my own demise; but I can assure you I only did it *once*. Alright I did it *twice*, but who's counting.

I would only add my negative feelings about the lack of necessity with the whole "online" status. It was always highlighted in a bold blinking "can't be missed" red that, quite frankly, might have been beautiful to wear...but not to stare at. It was *less* than subtle in its announcement of his blatant brush off and could only have been designed by a *sick* sadist, of whom I would *personally* like to meet one day for a good old-fashion *ass* kicking.

I left the clique crowd back in my school days, and that was *more* than a long time ago. Actually, I found *little* use for them then. However, somehow, these site developers had managed to harness that hopelessness of the odd man out. In some weird twilight zone twist, it made me feel as if *I* was the *only* one on the playground without peers. It's not like putting myself on this playground in the first place, wasn't grueling enough. The flashbacks of waiting to be picked for a team in gym class are *hardly* what I would call fond memories, and I *certainly* don't wish to repeat them. What's with this popularity protocol anyway? I was looking for a date not trying to out-number the flirts and friends of the other women residing in Eastern Michigan.

The 21st century may see winks, flirts and friend requests as cute must have's to meet someone, but it's simply unnecessary. If as an adult, you cannot formulate a sentence or two to introduce yourself and as the recipient of said sentence or two, you *cannot* respond, then all hope is lost. This is just my opinion, and we *all* know what they say about those.

The 21st century society has been taken over by SMS, IMs, text messages and emails, and now we are getting *so* lazy we can't even do *that* anymore. There's nothing more primitive than a small yellow smiley, depicting my wink...even if it *is* animated. I'd like to know where I can put in my official request to forgo the virtual flirts and friend requests. It's the pond scum of emails. What's next...virtual sex? Oh wait, we *already* have that.

Chapter 4

Bait and Switch:
Isn't there a law against that?

"Imagine a world, where we are the person we tell people we are...scary isn't it."

Don't waste the space: Leave a physical trait, personality malfunction or vice you would never admit to before meeting...come on you know you have one!

I had finally set up my first date. He was handsome and funny; he totally cracked me up on Yahoo. Yahoo, ugh that is a *whole* other chapter. He typed often about how important keeping in shape was to him and how *"in"* to exercise, he was. It was so obvious by his pictures that he had spent ample time in the gym, which is why his latest picture had become my official screen saver. To put the frosting on the cake to my match, he loved literature and drove a Mustang, *just* like me. I was more than a *little* excited at the prospect of meeting this perfect man for me.

Sifting through my boring closet of clothes, I gave up and headed to the store in search of the perfect find that would surely impress my date. First impressions are *everything.* I was going to make *certain* that my clicks, rejections and hours spent online searching for him, wouldn't be in vain. Indeed I was going to leave a lasting first impression. In fact, he was going to be so impressed, that he would be running home to delete his— no longer necessary— profile.

Pulling up to the Pub at least a half-hour early, I picked the table closest to the window in my enamored effort to watch him saunter across the lot. Alright, so it was *more* in my control freak fanatical way of judging how long I'd be staying. It's all about comfort, and *nobody* wants to be the one judged during that two-minute walk to the table. This is why, I was *completely* perplexed when this gentleman—I use the term loosely—sat himself down across from me. Who *was* this stranger in my booth? And more importantly, I hope he leaves before Mr. Perfect for me arrives! It was then this man smiled and introduced himself with a rather ridiculous rendition of "hello my name is" followed by his Yahoo id. "This *can't* be." He wasn't even *remotely* close to the man I'd been speaking to.

As he began struggling to squeeze himself in to my booth, his well developed beer belly bumped against the table and knocked over my drink. It was apparent that he was *quite* comfortable with the delusional image he had of himself, as evidenced by the fact that he showed up at all. And apparently, he was *just* as comfortable exposing it to me. While I realize "exposing" may seem like a dramatic word to use, it was *more* than an appropriate description for this scenario. Honestly, the shock of it all made my head spin and felt more like a flasher had sat down across from me—*with* an open coat—than a man I had made a date with.

As I regained my composure, from my impending panic attack, I took a sip from what was left of my drink. I was trying *desperately* not to appear rude, all the while amazed at his bullshit story about— well—basically his *entire* life. It was then that it dawned on me that he was the *same* man, who I had just seen from the window, getting dropped off by a friend. Apparently, his Mustang was in the shop and *apparently* he believed my intellect was in the shop as well. At this point, however, I'm starting to wonder if I had *any* intellect to begin with. Oh sure, I know this setup wasn't my fault, but *why* the hell was I *still* sitting there? As I tried to bring myself back to focus, I thought I could vaguely recognize the man from the pictures, but I still wasn't certain. Then again, at *that* point, I wasn't sure of much. For a brief moment, I *actually* thought I had been "punked" by a friend, as I surveyed the bar looking for the camera's.

I would *love* to know the thought process behind the bait and switch singles. Do they really think the ten years or that fifty-pound discrepancy will go unnoticed? Do they assume you will be *so* taken by their peachy personality that you'll overlook these "insignificant" facts? What reactions are they waiting for, when the picture they sent you wasn't even *them* to begin with? I don't understand what part of someone's brain reasons these ridiculous scenarios?

The Bait and Switch scenario is *always* the same—so I've experienced and been told—but in different calibers depending on gender. Men tend to bend the truth about height, living situations, weight and often times what they are looking for. Women out rightly *lie* about their body type, their kids or the fact that they're *nuts*. Don't assume I'm being judgmental here. The fact is, people lie. That's *not* judgment; it's merely the online code of conduct...lying that is. All I ask is that you present to me who you *really* are *before* we meet and give me the opportunity to agree to a date or run like hell.

While I agree that a mental connection is major, you cannot discount the fact that physical appeal is *paramount*, and while "It's what's on the inside that counts" may be the politically-correct thing to say...it's *bullshit*. Don't get me wrong it matters but *comes on*, be reasonable. I have found that those words are usually spewed by those who would perpetrate a "Bait and Switch" to begin with. *Yes*, I said perpetrate...it's a criminal act as far as I'm concerned. Men didn't always deem me physically acceptable dating material, but eventually I learned to pull my big girl panties up and *deal* with it.

At the *very* least, shouldn't these imposters of the internet be banned from the bandwidth? Where are the regulations? What happened to the "*All* powerful online Oz," who, up until now, had dictated the direction of my online experience? While I realize, a bitch-fest on the same site that's supposed to find you love, seems a bit contradictory, *shouldn't* there be a place where the conned can congregate? We need to be able to expose the fraudulent for who they really are. Who they are, that's laughable. You know these thieves of honesty have done it more than once, based on their comfort level *alone* when meeting you. I'm certain some have rogue "dishonesty" rap sheets longer than Lindsay Lohan, with the hopes that *someone* will actually stick.

With over *six* billion people in the world, I'm sure there's someone for everyone, at least I'm holding out hope for that. Online dating is hard enough, minus the bait and switch bonehead sinking it to a *new* level of less than fun in the dating arena. To me, it's the equivalent of schizophrenia gone wild Match.com style...who will I be *today*?

I'm sure I appear extremely harsh in this category of courting in the 21st century. Try not to judge me until you have sat a minute in my booth with "Mr. Oh So Wrong." My story here is not unique; it's been repeated time and time again. I have sat through *many* dates that might not have amounted to the ultimate connection. Those dates, however, definitely provided me with some pretty damn funny "Bait and Switch" stories. It's always easier to laugh at someone else's demise in the dating arena, or maybe it's laughter from the relief of knowing *I'm* not the only one.

Chapter 5

Thick or Thin:
Defining my body type by *his* standards

"Beauty is in the eye of the beholder...the tricky part is finding someone to behold you."

Don't waste the space: Leave your must-have physical traits list...is there enough space?

S kinny and fat were the less than diplomatic words we used to describe the female physique back in day. There were *no* in-between's. You were never classified as curvy or voluptuous, petite or a spinner. You were either the much sought-after skinny girl or the less than fabulous fat girl. Incidentally, I barely noticed physique critiques when *I* was skinny...imagine that. In the 21st century, however, we've politely replaced those words—like everything else in society—with our politically-correct equivalent. Usually, I'm *all* about trashing the politically-correct trend, but since I haven't seen skinny since my twenties, I'm good with it.

Today, we neatly place ourselves in categories *much* more complimentary...thanks to online dating. I would argue that it's *really* only complimentary if you fit into *two* of the five categories offered though. Understanding the physical attribute pyramid is con- fusing at best. Just when you *think* you understand it, it changes. It appears that body type has cycles much like fashion. Last season's run-way was sporting mini-skirts with leggings and small butts, but this season it's skinny jeans with junk in the trunk.

It's one thing to be trendy with clothes, but when the trends in a body shape changes, you're *pretty* much screwed. It's not like I can afford a butt lift and a boob job, and even if I *could*, what the *hell* would I do with them when the body trend changed...*again*? Maybe it's nature's way of evening out the playing field from time to time. I just hope my trend swings back around *before* I'm in my sixties.

Allow me to break it down in dating dialect, since these are the customary offerings from dating sites *all* around the globe, minus my sarcastic narration of course...which by now you should be getting *more* than used to.

♂♀

Slender: Better known as the spinner.

Average: The *average* portion of the population...no pun intended.

Few extra lbs.: Basically, you're fat.

Curvy: Big boobs and big butts...rolls are *not* included.

Athletic: Fantastically fit...hey, if he likes a girl that can kick his ass, who am *I* to judge?

♂♀

It's been my experience that *nobody* wants to put "A few extra pounds." In fact, in my years of online dating, I believe I've only seen it once. I had, however, witnessed *many* profiles in poundage denial. Here's a silver lining, it's better than saying, "I'm fat." What about our inclination at using the word "average?" Well let's face it, *not* an appealing account of who I want to be. Average is just so blasé. It's like saying, "Hey, don't look at me; I look like every other girl." Alas, I would suggest that *many* men would comfortably constrain *most* women into that category.

Is the whole "body type" breakdown *really* even necessary to begin with? I already have photos of myself, shouldn't that be enough? The internet and in particular online dating, is *full* of deception. I'm thinking having to check a box titled "A few extra pounds," *isn't* going to persuade a bait and switcher to "Do the right thing." In fact, I know it doesn't, based on the amount of "Bait and Switcher's" I've bumped in to.

The men have afforded me many chuckles at the "athletic" status on *their* profiles, when their beer bellies were *thee* predominant factor in their pictures. Word to the wise, "athletic" does *not* mean tossing the football around on a

Sunday once a month with the boys *or* wearing the latest Red Wings hat from your last event. Don't think I'm picking on you gents. In truth, the women are *no* better. One would think we are *all* average, based on our use of that box when filling out our profiles. Apparently *"average"* means anything from a size ten to a size twenty. Seriously, ladies, "average" does not mean the average size of our obese nation. How convenient, that we would factor in our fat, thereby classifying it as the status quo and deeming it as "average." Of course, online dating is not *exactly* what I would call reality. I guess if you want to check the "average" box...*go* for it. In fact, to *hell* with them all...check "athletic."

To break down these descriptions further, so we are all on the same presentation page; I've taken the liberty of compiling his and her definitions of the female physique. I can assure you, I *didn't* pull these from a hat. In fact, they were direct descriptions from many men and a *plethora* of powwows with the girls. Remember, over three years of research. Did I say research? I meant dates.

♂♀

Slender (Her):	Slim enough to avoid "muffin top" in a size 7 and under.
Slender (Him):	Better known as the spinner, she's thin enough to be spun for fun in the bedroom.
Average (Her):	Slim enough to avoid "muffin top" in a size 10-14.
Average (Him):	Not fat enough to embarrass him when introduced to his boys, but not *quite* what he was hoping for in the long run. In truth, she'll *probably* only be around until he finds his next spinner.

Few Extra Lbs.(Her):   Definitely a muffin top, but her personality shines!

Few Extra Lbs.(Him):   Yeah, that would be a *no*.
(Chubby Chasers are exceptions to the rule.)

Curvy (Her):   Overall voluptuous. Marilyn Monroe comes to mind.

Curvy (Him):   Booty *and* boobs. Must be a Jennifer Lopez look-alike and *nothing* less.

And drum-roll please...the much sought after...

Athletic (Her):   Toned in *all* the right places

Athletic (Him):   She likes sports. Oh...and she is built like a brick shithouse.

♂♀

Don't kill the messenger. *Trust me*, I'm not happy with my dating description of "average." I truly struggled with the whole "body type" format and at one point, made it my life's goal to be able to check the "athletic" box. Nevertheless, much like the luck I've had finding "Mr. Right," so too has the athleticism box evaded me. I'd have to say that many have just as difficult a time as *I* do deciding where to place themselves. The evidence was clear that we were all struggling by the stark differences of pictures posted and boxes checked. Unfortunately, many sites won't let you finalize your profile *without* the box checked. Oh, there were some sites that were kind enough to place a "Prefer not to answer" option...like *that* would help.

The fact is, whether I check that box *simply* because I didn't know *where* to place myself or I didn't want to answer, it would most certainly be misconstrued to mean "If I tell you the truth you won't email me." "Prefer not to answer," would have weeded me out of the dating garden, faster than a sixteen-year-old on his first date. I for one have had *enough* body image issues in *real* life, without having to confront them in a written format.

The whole concept is *quite* subjective, in my opinion. What someone else sees as "slender," I may see as an eating disorder and what another might see as "a few extra pounds," I may consider grossly obese so really...*what's* the point?

I always knew men were visual, but I don't think I realized exactly *how* visual they were. Sometimes I wonder if this visual trait is a scientific fact or just a conspiracy devised by the male species, for men to behave badly. Body size is, however, apparently *thee* most important detail for most men. I couldn't ignore this fact as this particular subject took precedence in *every* single conversation I've had since online dating.

There wasn't *one* man who agreed to meet me prior to peppering me with inquiries as to my actual size. Most men showed no restraint in their line of questioning either. "What size do you wear?" I can say now, that I am quite comfortable exposing the answer to that question..."I wear a size 10." I was, however, shell-shocked the first time a man asked me that. What happened to the rule of thumb, *never* ask a woman her age or her weight?

In the beginning, my handling of this situation was quite different. I figured if *he* had the balls to ask me that question, I was *well* within my rights for an all out verbal assault. It is my stance, that due to the shock of that question, a shock-ing response was *fair* game...just say-in. Eventually, I realized that line of questioning had *somehow* become a basic male pro-tocol in the dating world, and if I didn't bend I would be left boyfriend-less. It wasn't easy, but I succumbed and lovingly embraced my "average" self-analysis.

I have to add, that although I've adapted to the necessity of this vital information, I never *really* understood it. It didn't seem to matter how my profile described me or how many pictures I uploaded, there was always a need for more. *More* self-analysis, *more* descriptions, *more* detail and for extra security—I'm sure—a request for *more* pictures.

I will say, at least in this interrogation process I was forced to become more comfortable in my own skin. It didn't change the fact that I still hated that they asked though. It was hitting below the female belt and was the equivalent of asking him for his penis size. Some might argue the answer to *that* question is quite subjective as well. Of course, I'm sure he'd be all too happy to oblige your request...with a picture. Boy, if that isn't another needed chapter, I don't know what is!

Chapter 6

You've Got Mail, a Text, an IM
Becoming obsessed with our virtual world

"My patience has left the building"

Don't waste the space: Leave a story about what you did today that didn't include technology, any story...put down your phone!

It is nobodies intention to become hooked up to technology and intravenously fed life. Subject yourself to the addictive workings of the www and your quest for kinship too often, however, and you'll find yourself incapable of breathing without it. To think we used to function with snail mail, land lines and chance encounters. I sometimes wonder if the rise in divorce isn't a direct reflection of our technological *so-called* advances. Actually, I take it back; I *don't* wonder...I'm *certain* that it is. At the drop of a dime we can meet up, make-up and break up with little to no effort, real communication or *even* emotions for that matter.

It wasn't long after I had exposed myself to online dating, that I found myself syncing to every conceivable component to reveal the relationship I *thought* I was waiting for. Syncing was vital in receiving those all-important alerts. You know the ones...new message, new friend request, new flirt. They flashed on the screen of my Smart phone like an S.O.S. and held the key to my possible soul-mate...how could I *not* stay synced.

The more online dating I did the less patient I became. Surely, I couldn't *wait* to check my inbox until I made it home. If I waited *too* long, he might move on to someone else, due to my untimely response. Online dating was as quick paced as the stock market and *just* as volatile. The stock may be up for a little while, but if you wait *too* long to sell, you're likely to lose your investment.

My mother always told me, walking with my head held high would highlight my self-confidence; and I did follow that wise advice...*until* I started online dating that is. It was then, that I found myself starting to develop and awkward and indeed defeating habit, although at that time, I couldn't see it. Of course, I didn't *see* much during that time...overall. I was *constantly* walking around with my head pointing down, furiously typing an *urgent* something, to an *essential* someone, with little regard to the reality that surrounded me. How was I supposed to meet anyone in public if *all* they saw was the top of my head and *all* I ever saw were my feet?

The obsessive need and ability to be connected at all times is the number one defect with online dating. It's *too* easy! It's pretty compelling evidence that this connection is an addiction, when your date is logging in to check his new mail *before* he even makes it to his car post date. Another solid argument to point out addiction is when you're willing to forgo an evening out with your girlfriends, just so you can afford the next month of membership fees. I will readily admit that in the beginning, I too was constantly searching. Although in my defense, I must point out that at least I waited until I got *home* from my date...for the love of God. When I think of the hours I have lost, sitting in front of my computer screen typing in keywords to find him...hell, I could have written *four* books by now.

From time to time, I would try to break my addiction by deactivating or deleting my profile and ignoring the internet all together. Occasionally, I would manage to find the wherewithal to swear off the swindling that *is* online dating...for good. Sadly, I think the longest I could bare to stay away was two months. Eventually, the loneliness or sometimes simply boredom would grab hold of me, and I would recreate myself yet again by building yet *another* new profile.

Time and the virtual world I was residing in certainly took its toll over time as well. My optimistic "looking for" list was eventually replaced with my *very* unoptimistic "This is what I'm *not* looking for" list...as if *that's* the change that would make all the difference. It's a wonder anyone contacted me at all with all of that anger strewn across my page. I really believe, the pessimistic list only made me a bigger target... just for the sheer challenge of it all.

Rather than admit that I too had an addiction, I would merely convince myself that there just wasn't enough of a connection, or I wouldn't feel a need to check my mail, search new profiles or check the status of an earlier interest. In retrospect, it's not such a far-fetched idea, that there's little effort put forth in the new format for dating if all anyone has to do is turn on their Smartphone and login. Are our Smartphone's really *ever* off to begin with? At his/hers and my fingertips, were a plethora of prospects for the picking at all times, and it often times left *this* damsel a *little* more than distressed.

As time waned on, my addiction to search the sites changed from "Whose new today" to "Where is he?" My curiosity had eventually been replaced with escort exhaustion. Are you confused by the word "escort?" Don't be—I'm not suggesting I was an escort—but it's pretty much how these perpetual dates were starting to make me feel. I can tell you this. Men didn't seem quite as exhausted as me, as evidenced by that *bitch* of a blinking "online" sign, that although I hated, I signed in to see. This compulsive need for the next-best thing is a terrible trend and is making us look more like A.D.D. adults than serious searchers.

Eventually, my obsession to surf the singles scene via *every* technological avenue available to me was finally broken...*man* what a process. I realized that knowing what I know now, happenstance was a much more appealing option and *certainly* more sane. It just became so unappealing to subject myself to the vicious circle of trust traitors, who weren't able to break the beaten path of "You've got mail." Oh I'll admit that from time to time, I would log in simply for the sake of feeling like I was being proactive on my continuing search; but the effort or even the belief that "Mr. Right" could be found there was gone.

I knew that my experiences both from *my* behavior and the behavior of others made online dating a non-viable option. I would *never* be able to trust someone I had found online. There would always be a lingering fear that he could simply make a new profile and continue his search, *just* in case something better came along. Some quite frankly, didn't bother; they just used the same-old profile. There was no easy way to identify who was *truly* a possibility for the ending to my "happily ever after" saga and who was full of shit. If he was new to online dating, you knew the curiosity factor would be *so* high that "the next-best thing" would certainly play a role in his decision-making process. If he had been doing it for a while, there was *no* guarantee, he could break his addiction.

It's almost comical to me how often I would hear people complain about the demise of this new style in dating. They would go *on* and *on* about how nobody took it seriously, and how much they despised the online avenue for finding their "one." Even so, somehow we all still remained single and plugged in. How are we *all* unhappy with the dating situation, but we were *all* still single? The math of it just *wasn't* adding up. Were we simply too exhausted to continue putting forth any effort? Were our expectations too high? Perhaps, our complaints were a mere cover-up, disguising the façade of wanting to find someone, so we had an excuse for our addictions?

I can say one thing with *absolute* certainty; it can be construed as advice or simply a warning. Obsessions come in many forms. For instance, you find yourself for- going a night out on the town with your friends to sit and sift through thousands of profiles. Perhaps, you stay home to catch up on your neglected notices of the day...as if you haven't already checked at *least* once. I would suggest, if you resemble those remarks, you have *much* bigger issues than being alone. If your iPhone is *never* in your purse or on your hip, but *always* in your hand, and you selected a special ring for those all-important emails highlighting your next possible date. Your humanness has been hacked and a trip to reality is *desperately* needed.

Chapter 7

I'm in a Relationship with Yahoo

"I'm not gullible...I'm a hopeless romantic in survival mode."

Don't waste the space: Leave your first dating Yahoo experience...then promptly put him/her on your block list.

I am cringing and sinking deeper into my chair as I place my fingers on the keyboard to start this chapter. It's a chapter that must be written for the sake of saving the dating race, but I *despise* the thought of it, *despise* the exposing of my naiveté. I have always prided myself on being an intelligent and strong woman, "AD" days aside. However, this chapter will unfortunately make me appear to be anything *but* wise.

So I continue with trepidation as I introduce you to the devils' minion...Yahoo. I'm convinced it was created with the *explicit* intent of dragging me down to the bowels of dating hell, where I found myself perpetually plugged in. I believed my alternate reality *was* my existence and in fact, for a time it was.

During my Yahoo "relationships," I became nothing more than an animated mannequin sitting for hours on end chatting about the things I'd like to do, instead of going out and doing them. If I wasn't chatting I was waiting to chat, and if I wasn't waiting I was rushing back from somewhere that I had rushed to, in an effort *not* to miss his sign-in. All the while, I was convinced that the man on the other end of AT & T's complicated network of cables was, in fact, *just* as engulfed in this make-believe relationship as I was.

Yahoo seemed the next logical online step in the dating cycle. It was an important step, where you went from email to an *actual* conversation. It wasn't exactly an "actual" conversation by *real*-world standards. However, in the virtual world, it was more of a real time conversation than painstakingly waiting for the 21st century's snail mail. It's hard to believe that email would be likened to a forty-four cent stamp and a few days wait, but in dating time, email took *too* long.

As fast as I could type, I could receive a real time response. Incidentally, I have Yahoo to thank for my 90wpm. It was *much* better than email, but not *quite* as good as the phone. It had become an apparent protocol on the dating playground seeing as one of the first questions you were inevitably asked was, "Do you Yahoo?"

In the beginning, I felt privileged to acquire his Yahoo id, believing that it might mean something, like I don't know ...maybe he was *actually* interested in me. Call me crazy, but I really believed that a man wouldn't dare dole out his id if he wasn't at the very least a *bit* intrigued.

In retrospect, you could say the same for serial killers. They are intrigued by their next victims in some capacity too...are they not? Just as a serial killer would dispose of his victims, my Yahoo id could easily be deleted and blocked when he tired of talking. I suppose that beats being found in a ditch...although I *did* have a few dates where I wasn't sure that I *wouldn't* be found in a ditch. Then there were those dates that I'd of *preferred* to be found in a ditch by mid-date.

There were so many online masquerades that should have been obvious to me, had my hopeless romanticism not gotten in the way. For whatever reason, I was constantly blinded by the belief that people wouldn't blatantly lie. I *truly* believed that everyone else was looking for love too. Somehow, I had concluded that if he put in time online, he *must* be seriously searching ...silly me. Keep in mind, when I say, "Time" I'm talking for *hours* on end.

It didn't take me long to make a mental note of the obvious red flags one inevitably gets while Yahooing. Once I recognized them, his instant messages were quickly replaced with his "instant" removal. Indeed, he would be added to what had become my growing friends' list of possibilities gone awry, marked...*blocked.*

Let's face it, not every swindling single is as suave as the next, which afforded me the ability to break down the deception, on some occasions rather quickly. Perhaps I'm not *completely* stupid after all. I recant that statement, to the contrary, when it came to Yahoo, *stupidity* was my middle name.

I *will* give myself major kudos for at least recognizing when I was hooked up to a hidden agenda. If his first words typed were babe, baby or sexy...chat time *abruptly* ended. Although there will be a chapter covering those less than poetic pet names, let me just say now that no decent man looking for a respectable woman is going to pass out a pet name before she types her first sentence.

Next in the liar line of Yahoo's relationships, would have to be photo-sharing. When the first sentence he sends is "Do you want to see more pictures," I can tell you now your answer should be a resounding *no*. Unless, of course, he's your cousin Ned, who has just moved to some foreign land and wants to share his new surroundings with you.

It has been my experience that passing pictures Yahoo style, is nothing more than code for a colorful collection of his non-clothed self. While at times I found humor in this half attempt at seducing me, for the most part, it bored me. It was just so *incredibly* disrespectful and the more it happened, the more it pissed me off...which means I was pissed off *a lot*.

However, the mother of all makeshift Yahoo relationships was undoubtedly the cam. The first time I was requested to cam with someone I excitedly accepted. I thought the request meant he was more than likely the *real* deal I had been waiting for. Someone wouldn't expose themselves visually if they *weren't* serious *would* they? I would surmise if they weren't seriously trying to get off...no probably not. Again, this isn't a guess; this is experience at its finest...believe me when I say, I wish it was a guess.

Often times I could be caught camming alone, although not by choice. Indeed, I was always greatly disappointed, as I listened to yet *another* explanation of how his cam was on the fritz. I realize at this point I'm not next in line for any intellect award. In fact, my ridiculous reasoning would better suit me as a comical caricature in Mad Magazine, depicting me with a wide-eyed, quizzical look as the pervert on the other end streams endless amounts of nakedness across my screen. Hopeless romanticism always made me look like *such* an ass.

On five separate occasions, that ranged from one month to more time than I care to admit to, I sat typing my heart out to someone I *thought* might be special. I didn't jump to this conclusion all on my own...although with my naiveté you really couldn't put even *that* past me. All of that aside, my feelings were inevitably taken hostage as I was fed the lines I needed to hear by the—dare I say—bastards that played these Yahoo games. I won't argue that my hopeless romanticism was the precursor that made it *easy* for me to believe and even easier for them to take advantage of me, but it wasn't the *only* factor in these fictitious relationships.

Somehow, these five managed to escape from my rigorous removal process, allowing them to make it to their *next* level of lies. I'm beginning to realize that hopeless romanticism isn't something to be admired, but something to be admonished...in *particular* in me. This fairytale philosophy had brought me to tears on more than *one* occasion and seemed to play with my perception of reality...*often*.

These five were masters in their craftiness at deception to say the least. You would think I'd of learned after the first "the jokes on me," but they were always upping the ante. Each one threw something into the mix to meander my misgivings from my last Yahoo messenger mistake. They were cunning in their collection of heart-wrenching love gone wrong dramas to pull me into their virtual world too. There *always* seemed to be a fitting story about the quest for their queen that would turn into a traumatic ending for them. Unfortunately, I bit the bait *every* time.

The stories from these deceivers were certain to end with one of the three D's; death, divorce or deception. It was an apparent popular online messenger game and *I* was usually on the losing end. It's almost as if they had studied the female psyche and could permeate that protective layer where a woman's nurturing genes reside. Unfortunately, once they broke the barrier, it was easy for them to have their virtual way with me.

I would like to say, in the essence of not appearing *completely* ignorant, that my Yahoo relationships didn't *always* stay in a typed format. Indeed, many times phone calls followed the chat sessions, and offline dates were inevitably set ...but broken. Of course, I realize *now* that those dates made were bound to be broken, and they amounted to nothing more than an evil plan. They were an ingenious cover-up, engineered to ease my growing concerns—but more importantly—to make me *shut* my mouth. These men knew their intentions from the get go. They were never going to meet me at all...*ever*.

It all makes sense...right? How could I get angry if he missed his flight back into town, when he made it a point to login and let me know? Wouldn't it be *rude* of me to be less than understanding about the death of his stepfather, mother or father? If he suddenly felt nervous about my acceptance of him in person, only because I am *so* beautiful, should I be angry or feel flattered that he's placed me on that pedestal? I felt like a referee between my intellect and my female let me fix it side. What *was* it about me that was *always* willing to be left waiting, as long as *he* was left feeling better about the fact that he had to cancel our date? Oh sure there were times my brain actually had a say, but it was *often* a losing battle to my heart. It simply would be too much for my heart to admit that I actually *was* the moronic miss-manager of my love life that my boisterous brain kept telling me I was.

I'm certain there are many that are reading this particular chapter and thinking to themselves "What an *idiot* I would *never*." However, I feel equally confident in the idea that there are many more who are now breathing a *significant* sigh of relief, knowing they *weren't* the only ones. I may have been naive with the net, but I know, in no uncertain terms, that I am *not* alone on the yellow brick Yahoo road...I've just got the balls to admit it. I'm certain that there are also those that want to hear the meat and potatoes of these less than real relationships. I'm happy to announce that you should be more than pleased as you peruse the chapter reserved strictly for *those* experiences. Although, something tells me that you aren't going to believe them even when you *do* finally get to read about it...God knows *I* still don't.

Here's your moral for this chapter. Feel free to Yahoo your yearning heart away. However, be sure it's *after* you get his name, number and a date that *doesn't* include you in your pajamas, with a glass of wine and the soft glow of your computer screen.

Chapter 8

When I Asked for a Picture...
I meant of your face

"Just when you think you can't take another second of it...you manage to."

Don't waste the space: Print out and tape a picture of your first sexting freak here...oh come on you know you have one!

I'm thinking the title of this chapter speaks for itself, at least if you've dipped your toes into the dating pool within this century. However, just in case you *don't* know what you're missing, let me assure you that today's tech-savvy singles will make sure you *don't* miss much. As always, I write from my perspective, which means the caveman will take the club *again*...in the head that is. Of course, I'm not ignorant to the initiatives of some woman as well. In other words, the pendulum swings both ways, even in *this* category. In fact, the more I write and retrospect the more I'm starting to believe Mars and Venus aren't so different after all...contrary to what we've been told. We may not speak the same language, but I'm thinking the old adage; "Actions speak louder than words"...apparently *not* so old.

I'll *never* understand how the male psyche reasoned the scenario, "Send her a picture of your package...she'll *love* it." However, on most occasions, I had barely finished saving his name into my contact list, before a text or an email of his phallus was flying at me faster than the speed of light.

While I am *hardly* what you would call a modest individual—after my experience with childbirth and twenty some-odd years of sexual encounters—this particular male move even managed to shock *me* most of the time. It didn't help that the sender was less than selective about when he sent either. Is there really ever an appropriate time *to* press send in this scenario?

Sitting at my parents for coffee and...incoming penis pictures. Standing in the line at the grocery store and ...imagine that, more penis pictures. At parent-teacher conferences and...*you* guessed it, another penis picture. Whatever happened to leave a little to the imagination? Was it *only* reserved for the female gender? And if so, how did even *women* get sucked into this sexting world?

It always struck me as odd that the male species would sacrifice themselves to the female masses. It's no secret that penis size is paramount with the caveman class. I would think he would be a *bit* more concerned that his manhood might not measure up.

Think about it gentlemen; that penis picture could be a deal breaker, instead of a relationship maker. And if it was a one-night stand you were hoping for, it's my stance you should *definitely* forgo the phallus photograph. If, however, you simply *can't* withhold your want to hit send, it should be required at the *very* least, that he tagged his pictures with a note that specifies... "Object in the picture is smaller than it appears." The gig is up guys. Women know *all* about the close-up camera shots and the optical illusions they create, which is why we wouldn't be caught *dead* in one.

I realize it will appear as though I'm speaking out of both sides of my mouth in this next paragraph. Think what you may, but in the end you'll realize that it's *really* not the case at all. It's was more an unintentional, self-induced misuse of my nurturing side. On the rare occasion, a man would actually *ask* if I wanted that particular picture, I didn't always have the heart to tell him no. Of course, most of the time, asking was omitted from the get go.

It wasn't out of interest or even the need for another laugh that I accepted, but out of empathy. I believe the penis *is* the male identity—though I suppose I could be wrong—but with all of these penis pictures flying around, I suggest my theory *is* correct.

Armed with this thought, I couldn't bear to break his ego. Of course, once he hit send his digits were bound for deletion followed by a block on my Verizon account. Nevertheless, for that moment, I felt I spared his masculinity. Whatever came after that didn't matter because *he* could no longer ask, and *I* no longer had to answer. I suppose in my "AD" days it was much more acceptable for me to acknowledge such crude conduct, but once I was *seriously* searching...dick pics were a deal breaker.

The whole sexting trend started to become rather depressing. It was becoming painfully apparent, that the probability of finding "Mr. Right" was rapidly decreasing, the more pictures I received. This particular epiphany made me see that tall, dark and handsome were trite objectives when compared to the bigger picture, and suddenly genuine and good hearted became the goal. I had no idea, that finding those character traits would be harder than climbing Mt. Everest...barefoot *and* blindfold.

I'll never forget the first picture I received. At the time, I assumed it was a random event and it left me in a state of teen-like embarrassment. I didn't *dare* save it. What would I do if someone saw it? I wanted to tell my bff, but I had many reservations and fear that she might see it as *my* fault...*especially* with recollection of my "AD" days. I knew my lack of demanding respect would be construed as encouragement on my part. I suppose maybe it was, but it wasn't intentional.

The next few I received were met with a "Geeze this is becoming a trend" attitude, as I tossed more and more pictures into my techno trash can. The constant barrage of phallus features had become quite annoying, and honestly, a bit boring as well. Though I *definitely* can't say, "If you've seen one you've seen them all," the novelty was wearing thin. I had no interest in seeing them all or even *one* more.

I convinced myself that I was picking the wrong men and adjusted my criteria to appeal to a more appropriate mate. I actually formulated a list of red flag words and behaviors in my effort to weed them out, but to no avail. It didn't seem to matter *how* many times or to *whom* I requested the "Opt out" of penis pictures. They just kept coming like pilgrims attempting to hoard the newly found land. I'm still not sure exactly *what*, in the mind of man, this had to do with courting; but it seemed better suited to an animalistic mating ritual, than a precursor to a date.

It wasn't until I met a Christian man who professed his need for a dignified, God fearing woman before blasting me with his bareness, that I thought this was *definitely* the trend in online dating. However, it was when I admitted my "dick dilemma" to a close friend—and we spent an hour viewing her rather large collection of penis pictures on her phone—that I realized it had surpassed trend and moved into the epidemic arena.

For a while, my bff and I started to store said photographs. They were neatly organized in folders, according to manhood make-up...for the laugh-ability factor when pow-wowing with the girlfriends. Sometimes, it was just for a general pick-me-up. I could never seem to beat them...no pun intended. Instead, I joined them, in a manner of speaking. It was my effort to humor myself; what can I say?

There was the "Teeny Peeny," I'm sure you get the connotation. The "Male Monstrosity," *definitely* a cause for penis envy among the cavemen. The "Euro," for the circumcised challenged and the list goes on. I fully realize this seems a bit on the immature side for a forty something female, but I'm not going to apologize for this minuscule misbehavior. It was something to laugh at when the chips were down and when online dating, the chips were *usually* down. I can't help but wonder with amusement right now; how many men are rethinking their rushed responses to "Can you send me a picture" after reading *that* paragraph.

This chapter certainly wouldn't be complete without a discussion of the requests for returning the rendezvous into picture porno land. More shocking than the pictures received, *had* to be the adamant demands that *I* reciprocate in these mating rituals of the 21st century. In the essence of honesty, there was a time a two when my arm was twisted to the point of no return, forcing me to partake in the plundering of said land...to a *small* degree. Furthermore, I am *only* admitting this to avoid the "This is what she *didn't* tell you" scenario, just in case this book ever *actually* gets published. Unfortunately, that means what you think it means.

Yet again, I must hang my head in shame while writ- ing this book. Right, wrong or indifferent, you can be sure it was *only* in a moment of weakness, and *always* involved my heart that allowed me to be coerced. I never said it wouldn't come back to bite me in the ass...case in point. Understand, of course, that this *time* or two had *nothing* to do with my heart in the typical sense. In other words, it wasn't about feelings for someone, but about becoming disheartened with the whole online dating scenario. There was definitely a time, when I simply gave up on the idea of anything even remotely close to a real relationship and gave in to his groveling. Just, another *not* so proud moment in the life of.... Boy, these *not* so proud moments are *really* beginning to add up...aren't they? At least I can stand tall in the knowledge that I have been honest...and omitting *is* dishonest.

As an online dating veteran—I *seriously* deserve a me- tal for surviving—it has come to my attention that men *are* visual. I would have to argue that nothing can replace the sexual surprise of a package gone un-opened, but I'm *sure* they'd disagree. Who'd of thought our mothers had it right when they said, "Why buy the cow if you can get the milk for free?" Maybe it's time that saying changes much like *everything* else in the 21st century. More apropos would be "Why buy the bull if you can get the horn for free?"

It's a travesty, but modesty and morals are not the only two mortalities in the death of dating. Alongside the grave of romance, I am *sure* to see my own epitaph one day, which will sadly and embarrassingly read: Here lies my private parts 1969–Send.

Don't waste the space: Keep a running tab on exactly how many porno pics you get...without asking!

Chapter 9

Do You Even Know My Name?

"If you want to be king, you have to earn the right to rule my kingdom—and knowing the queens name—kind of important."

Don't waste the space: Leave a list of usernames that called you everything but your name...refer to list often, online dating gets monotonous, it will help avoid repeat offenders!

I've been called many things in my life, some of which I'm not particularly fond of. Most often, they were spewed from a relationship gone bad. God knows I've had my fair share of *those*. I do, however, have a given name that I tend to use when meeting someone for the first time... imagine *that*. You wouldn't think that would be a strange concept...right? That's not to say that I haven't enjoyed a pet name a time or two in my life; but I *usually* reserved them for a man I'd known longer than five virtual minutes.

Pet names are another one of those cavemen reasoning's that I can't seem to wrap my brain around. I can tell you this, it ranks *pretty* high up on my personal list of "pet" peeves...pun intended. I wish I could say this annoying ritual was reserved for my younger male counterparts, but *once* again, the dating world has managed to mingle all ages into the same category with no hope of deciphering lines in maturity levels. I can't help but feel perturbed and a bit perplexed, by the *incessant* need for name calling. It begs the question, "Do you even know my name?" More often than not, they didn't. There was startling evidence to prove that, by the mere fact that I never got as far as "hello my name is" before I was branded with an over-used or offensive offshoot of *his* idea of a compliment.

Language is definitely the most profound gender gap when it came to online dating. In fact, it appeared more like the Grand Canyon than a mere gap. I tried to bridge the divide *many* times over by repeating my name. You know, just in case he missed it, but the pet names persisted. I think, over-all, women tend to misconstrue his meaning initially, thinking that *maybe* he's just *"in"* to me. However, to me, it started to have the same feel as that—*oh* so cute—winking smiley I sent as a flirt...un- necessary and annoying.

I suppose the fact that I was forever trying to reason away his less than evolved etiquette—be it pet names or penis pictures—was just a part of my genetic make-up as a woman.

I seemed too over-indulge in the overanalyzing department when it had *anything* to do with the intentions of men...as if *that's* an odd quality for a woman to have. Apparently, I felt it was my responsibility to "Give them the benefit of the doubt" and my optimistic attitude took a beating because of it. My *God* I have caused so much self-inflicted pain throughout this process.

I learned the hard way, just as I learned *everything* that had to do with online dating, that if I let *one* "sweetie" slip, it would be seen as a bite on the bait for him to go ahead and behave badly. It's been my experiences that pet-names were almost always a sure-fire sign that he *wasn't* a serious searcher, and if I played into his "vixen" cat call, I was *sure* to be his next victim.

At this point, I've probably become too cynical for even the not so delicate dating world of the 21ˢᵗ century. I will, however, stand firm that the following list should be reserved for a relationship that has sustained a *little* more than a Yahoo chat session or a drink at the local watering hole.

♂♀

Adorable, amazing, angel, babe, baby, baby cakes, baby doll, beautiful, boo, cougar, cupcake, cutie, cutie pie, darling, dear, delicious, diva, divalicious, doll, doll-face, girly, girly girl, gorgeous, honey, honey buns, hot mama, hot stuff, hottie, hun, lollypop, ma, MILF, peaches, precious, pretty thang, princess, pop tart, sexy, sweets, sweetie, sweet cheeks, sweet thang, sweetheart, sweetness, sugar, sugar mama and vixen...just to name a few.

♂♀

In fact, I'll expand on that last statement and suggest that there are some of these standard offerings that shouldn't be used at all...*ever*, case in point ...MILF.

For those that may not have an understanding of this acronym, allow me to educate you on its meaning. "Mothers I'd like to f#@k." I suppose the *entire* acronym should be found offensive, but quite frankly, the mother part *really* gets to me. It's as if I should pride myself on the fact that I've given birth and yet *somehow* I'm still found somewhat desirable by the sexually superior male species. Can you think of anything more insulting?

"Ma" was another monstrosity of a nickname. While it may seem I'm forming a pattern here on a possible distaste for motherhood, I can tell you I'm quite proud to hold that title. However, I'm *not* trying to be a mother figure for my interest, *nor* do I want to be seen as one in the bedroom...*total* turn-off.

To me, the premature pet name pattern should be likened to a frozen mixed bag of carrots, corn and peas. While each had an individual title and taste, they were forced into a bag together where they lost their individuality, thereby lumping them all together with the same tag...vegetables. Am *I* just another one of the lost identities in the bag of female veggies? Is it easier for men to generalize our gender in their effort *not* to mix up our names during their mating rituals of one-night stands?

I'm thinking that's giving the caveman *too* much credit. I would suggest, they simply see their pseudonym as a cute compliment that might suck her into the sack *that* much sooner. Speaking of premature pet names, you can be certain premature *anything* won't be found *anywhere* on my want list...just say-in.

In the end, I suppose I should be grateful that he's unwittingly showing his "player" card right out of the gate. At least, it affords me the opportunity to bow out quickly and painlessly. It's not so bad when I've denoted little more than a few keystrokes before kicking him to the curb. Don't get me wrong, it's not that I *wouldn't* appreciate a "sweet nothing" in my ear from the object of my affection. I just wanted to know his name first, and I'd of *liked* it, if he could remember mine.

Chapter 10

You Feel So Good:
I mean I feel good...I mean you feel...
Oh never mind!

"If you can't touch it and it can't touch you—it ain't real—no matter how good it feels."

Don't waste the space: Write down what an idiot you were for just doing that...I know you're relaxed now, but do it anyway!

Could the rituals of dating in the 21ˢᵗ century *be* any more disheartening than this chapter? I think not! We've managed to reduce our communication skills to pushing buttons and sending smiley animations, but who'd of thought we would be stupid enough to disregard the absolute *best* part of being human? I'm referring to intimacy and the intoxicating "O." Real experiences have been replaced with the supposed virtual equivalent of actually living every chance we get. Sadly, sex was not spared from our technological advances.

I'm not talking about your average porn site. God knows those have been around forever and will continue to be for centuries to come. However, I always thought those were reserved for the lonely or as stress relief...so my ex-husband used to tell me. That wasn't sarcasm that was a dig. God I *love* writing my own book. I had no idea online dating would include me becoming an unintended porn playmate for my online interest. I'm referring to those typed relationships that *somehow* manage to extend past a general conversation and transform into what we have come to believe *is* intimacy.

After what I've seen and shamefully done through- out this entire process, I'm convinced that intimacy is an inaccurate title for online anything. By the way, do not assume that's admittance in this category, but don't assume it's *not* either. Can a cam and a few keystrokes *really* be the definition of intimate? It seems in *this* century it can. We have become so detached from the real world and so entranced with our virtual worlds, that it has now become our reality.

Virtual sex is the topic of this chapter and a *much* sought-after commodity these days. The strong evidence in this trend is vast, simply by the amount of times I've been asked alone. Alone, now *there's* an appropriate account of what this technological advance has *really* achieved. I am *far* from a prude. I realize that there may be a time and a place for phone sex and the like; for instance, long distance relationships, post meeting in the real world and developing a relationship of course. Even the playful text, gearing him up to what he'll come home to later, *I* believe, is an essential aspect of a healthy relationship.

The difference in said scenarios is in the end-result of *real* human contact. You can't replace a consuming kiss, and you would be hard-pressed to replace the "All powerful O" that originates from a deep respect and love for another human being.

As a woman, I can understand the pull towards something that would allow her to hide her perceived imperfections. The right camera angle, proper lighting and positioning, God *knows* we've mastered the "make me look good" angles since the whole online experience exploded. Make believe that is so mastered, in fact, that we can conveniently hide the kid ravaged carnage we're *really* dealing with. However, isn't that *so* called carnage what makes us who we are? Wouldn't the right man want to see our life story and wouldn't he love us in spite of those imperfections anyway? Perhaps this is just another fairytale coming back to bite me in the ass for believing.

Can the cam really give a woman the closeness she so desperately needs...the closeness that we *all* desperately need as humans? Have we evolved past real passion, real people and real pleasure?

I can't predict the purpose of an online affair as far as men go, so I suppose I'll just pull the "visual" card out again for their behavior. I am, however, getting a *bit* tired of placing the blame on the same bullshit excuse. Have we really become so lazy that we can't even manage to have *real* sex anymore?

Unfortunately, the woman's movement has made women believe that we can have it all, *all* on our own, with the simple switch of the latest gadget on the market; but is that *really* all there is? I'm sure I just pissed off the feminists, but you can't argue the facts. We can vibrate our way to contentment, but that vibrator isn't going to buy you a Christmas present or care about your day.

Of course, he can look into your cam filled eye's post Yahoo coital and pretend he *wishes* he could cuddle, but is that *really* the same? Could there *be* a more empty feeling than shutting off your computer when play time is over? I'm starting to believe that we would rather pretend than partake in anything remotely real because then we wouldn't have to admit to our shortcomings, whether they be physical or in life as a whole. We wouldn't have to share our selves, to the point of exposing ourselves to the experience of disappointment, pain or rejection that a *real* relationship could entail.

Instead, we submerse ourselves in a sub-par world of unreality in search of something that simply does *not* exist ...perfection. And what, exactly, have we achieved then? In my opinion, nothing but hard wiring in our brains that the ideal is indeed perfect and that to accept anything less would be below our standards. Are any of us privy to perfection to begin with if it does exist?

As a woman, I can tell you the initial attraction to virtual sex *isn't* the end-result of the all powerful "O." Instead, it's the over-controlling need to be desired, and it's this genetic malfunction that manipulates the senses when it comes to online dating too. This whole sexual protocol for women can only lead to the demolition of any semblance of self, rendering many of us puppets in his pornographic play. It angers me that my DNA had gotten the better of me, and my intellect had caved to the cultured caveman and his cam. That's not to say that the initiation of an online sexual rendezvous was *always* done with malice. I'm sure it was occasionally nothing more than his over abundance of testosterone. The cam was merely the closest thing to a release of those hormones. However, my experiences and the stories I've been told certainly depict a more devious intention.

There is nothing more deceptive than drawing someone in with the image of "happily ever after" for a few moments of moans. Could there *be* anything more predator like, than preying on the promise of a tomorrow by an unsuspecting soul. I liken it to rape. Not in the conventional sense of course, but rape of the heart and besides what in any online relationship scenario could be considered conventional to begin with.

If you've ever seen the movie "Wall-E," then you might get the metaphor. I'm afraid Pixar presented us with a premonition of our future. We have become *ridiculously* reliant on widgets to get us through our day. Just like those characters, we too, live in a society where our technological advances have depraved us of even the most basic of human functions. For us, it's real-world communication, but for them, it was walking. Are we next? It may seem like hover-chairs that can provide us with everything we need *but* an orgasm is a far cry from reality, but then how real is virtual sex? I found it particularly ironic that Wall-E, which *is* the epitome of technology, falls in love; while the humans' continue the façade of an easier life.

Perhaps the future will entail a technology that somehow gets us to realize the value of a *real* not computerized connection. Maybe in this future, we will *stop* envying the stories that depict these connections and realize that we actually have the ability to achieve them...if we would just put down our phones, shut off our computers and look up.

Chapter 11

Liars, Players and Cheats Oh My
Defining 21st century datables

"A large beautifully wrapped box can suddenly become so unappealing once opened to reveal its content; while a small box with ordinary wrapping can be filled with the most amazing surprises."

Don't waste the space: Make a list of your "datable" character traits...yes you do have them.

The story of my experiences with online dating wouldn't be complete without a chapter breaking down the datables. If you want to limit the bumps and bruises you are certain to attain throughout this process, its important that you understand the many personas you will run across when attempting to online date. Actually, if you plan to date at *all* in the 21ˢᵗ century, it would behoove you to have these handy definitions.

Though some are tried and true with nothing more than a new 21ˢᵗ century title, there are others that have just recently made the scene, and sadly, I have met *all* but one. Keep in mind, this list depicts the most likely candidates you'll come in contact with, but in *no* way signifies all the fruit loops you might subject yourself to, especially when online dating.

The biggest mistake I have made through my dating debacles was to believe that if I loved hard enough, long enough, I could change a particular persona. Unfortunately, my optimism had a way of kicking me when I was down and the hardest thing about my "love harder" theory was the lesson I learned from it. By this point in the book, it should be obvious that my naiveté had gotten the better of me on *many* occasions.

I wish I'd of listened to my aunts' advice. "Screw me once shame on you, screw me twice shame on me." To date, it appears to be the soundest advice of my *not* so young life. Unfortunately, I didn't which is why there was a *perpetual* sign across my forehead that read, "Treat me like shit." Let's just say, I've shamed myself an awful lot when it came to my perception of how to acquire love through online dating.

It should be noted, that these datables many times are not gender specific. However, I can only give you my perspective on the male species, as I'm about as heterosexual as one can get. I have had the opportunity to *hear* about my side of the coin on many occasions, usually through male friends or horror stories told to me while on a date of my own. Sadly, on occasion, some of them could be found in my closest circle of sisters. Dare I say through my "AD" days, I fit into some of my *own* sinister categories as well?

I will suggest that most, like me, eventually *do* indeed morph into a much more acceptable version of being human. However, don't hang on hoping to be in his or her presence when and if the change does occur. To assume you will be the difference isn't hopeless romanticism or even optimism, it's *just* plain stupid. Let me assure you, that if you've heard the urban legend of the girl who got the guy, who up until her was the epitome of "the bad boy," it is either just that—a legend—or merely luck in timing.

I'm sure most have heard at one time or another that "You can't change a person." Well, I'm here to tell you that there are a *whole* lot of truths to that statement. I've tried every conceivable avenue to make someone fit, and I've kicked myself in the ass many times over because of it. The only power to make changes we have is to make changes in ourselves, which, quite frankly, you may *want* to do after reading this list. So without further ado, allow me to introduce to you...the datables.

♂♀

Mr. Bad Boy: He hasn't changed much over the years, but his description bears repeating, since the women tend to forget and fall for his "dangerous" disposition. He'll usually stick around for as long as you'll tolerate him and tolerating his lack of actually being around *is* the key. You can be sure you will always be left waiting ...waiting for a phone call, waiting for a return text or *hell* waiting for any other form of communication for that matter. You will never know when you will see him next, or for how long. He will keep you guessing where you stand with him, not because he doesn't want you to know, but because he doesn't stand with anyone.

He is a loner and you are lonely because of it. Your heart and sanity will be tested daily for the few kibbles of kindness; he'll throw your way. It's his hope that these kibbles will convince you that your undying devotion is indeed changing the error of his ways...remember "Screw me twice...." Most women will try one of these "bad boys" on for size at least once in their lives both for the challenge of changing him and the ability to let go of life's bothersome responsibilities. Regardless of his age or attitude, "the bad boy" will force you to let your hair down, but stay *too* long, and you'll go from crazy and carefree to just plain crazy.

Ms. Diva: Better known as "the bitch," she's a walking attitude and the female version of "the bad boy." The biggest gender bender in this persona is that he won't get kibbles of *anything* from her. She's a constant flow of teasing and insinuations that if he's at her beckon call, she may call on *him* at the end of the night. She'll stand at the bar and wait for the drinks to pour in, *all* at his expense just long enough for him to *think* he's made headway; then *she'll* be heading for the door. If she feels the need to feed her sexual hunger, and he's the recipient of her end of night surprise, he may count himself as "the lucky one." Nevertheless, he'll be left dreaming about the one that got away because he'll likely *never* hear from her again. It should be noted that many Divas are actually already taken, but they *love* the attention. Attachments don't stop this Ms. from enticing the entranced to do as she demands and his willingness to respond merely feeds her obnoxious ego.

Mr./Ms. Cheater: Not to be confused with "Mr./ Ms. Player," the cheater is *often* times married, *sometimes* dating or otherwise living with their significant other. They tend to lean towards courteous, and they usually suffer from "The Greener Pasture" syndrome (See next chapter.) Mr. Cheater tends to use the "*we*" word depicting a world of wonderfulness that he and she will share together, but *never* commits *too* far into the future. Ms. Cheater grabs his attention with her woes of a less than loving life with her mate. The only significant difference in this Mr. and Ms. is his innate ability to hide that he's hitched and her ability to feed off of the male ego. Of course, it's precisely this masculine DNA that makes the damsel in distress theatrics so effective. Do *not* be lured into believing that you will be his or her savior in *any* capacity. In the end, it's more than likely you'll wind up the rebound, and possibly run down by a significant other...should they find out.

Mr./Ms. Player: Almost always single but on the rare occasion taken, Mr. and Ms. Player are in it for the *sheer* numbers alone. They are usually suffering from "The Next-Best Thing" syndrome, but that's no excuse for their bad behavior. Charmers to their core, they have an uncanny knack for making you feel like you've won the prize, but all you're *actually* getting is a one-night stand. Almost always abnormally attractive and they have an agenda to fill...did I mention they were built to fill it. Of course, once the thrill of the kill is gone...you can expect you will be too. Never assume if he or she puts in some time with you, it means you're something special. Chances are you just haven't given up the goods yet. Mr. and Ms. Player *love* a challenging game and the only way to know what they are dealing you is to get the dish on how long their *last* King or Queen was in their deck of lies. If it looks more like a game of "Go Fish" you might want to put your line in a different pond.

mr. Cub: He's a young man on a mission, usually between the ages of twenty and twenty-five and seeking a woman at *least* ten years his senior. His opening line will almost always be "Age is just a number" or "Girls my age are game players, and they don't know what they want." These are supposed attraction tools to lure the trendy "Cougar" into his trap but in reality, the Cougar can't be lured, unbeknownst to the cute but oh *so* ignorant Cub. He's in it for the sexual experience of an older woman as they have become legends in their own right in the 21st century. Unfortunately, many Cubs get caught up in their first experience leaving them hooked for the rest of their young years with an addiction for more rather than just a fond memory. Can you say stalker? Eventually, mr. Cub will have to be happy that he's acquired some tools for his sexual toolbox and move on to a more appropriate mate.

Ms. Cougar: Contrary to what the male species believes about this particular persona, a true Cougar does not do the seeking...she is sought. She is seductive, sultry and the *hottest* commodity this century. The Cougar has almost always been through at least *one* marriage or long term union and oozes sexuality, usually because she has hit her sexual peak. It should be noted that a skankily dressed older woman, who ogles the Cubs at the bar or emails them on the net, does *not* a Cougar make. Going home with the first young man who will have you just makes you a slut. A true-blue Cougar is *nothing* but class and is selective in her sexual rendezvous. The Cub shouldn't be so certain she'll choose him, just because he's a young stud. It's imperative he realizes it isn't his strategy under the sheets that helps him win the prize; it's his stamina...sorry to bust your bubble boys.

Mr. Money Bags: He's been around for centuries and loves to intrigue the young ladies with his arsenal of goods. Mr. Money Bags is *all* about the arm candy and makes no bones about it. He'll spoil the object of his current affection and show her off like the trophy that she is...on the outside anyway. Unfortunately, he is usually left standing alone before too long, as in this category "Age *is* a number"...at least in Ms.

Gold-digger's eyes. These young women will collect as many goods as they can before they retire this geriatric gent to his antique shelf for the next sister Gold-digger to come along, unless of course, his years are numbered.

Ms. Gold-digger: There are two categories for this Ms. First is the young ditzy digger. She seeks out the oldest most loaded man, sinking her claws in deep as, she bides her time. It's her hope that she'll be digging a hole for him sooner rather than later, and it beats digging into his crotchety old pockets. If he's got more time than she has to spare, she'll take what she can get before she goes on to the next money maker who's itching for a trophy to polish. Ms. Gold-digger II wouldn't sink to the level of an old man. She's in it for the long haul. Beautiful and more plastic than a Barbie Doll, this digger is sure to seek out a young and attractive man. He is usually a self-made money maker or was well fed with a silver spoon. Ms. Gold-digger II takes him *all* the way down the aisle, where she is certain to live in luxury *with* or *without* love. What she lacks in love for her mate, she's sure to make up for with his money. Sadly, by the time he catches on to her dollar sign addiction, he must grin and bear her cash consumption or divorce her and give it to her anyway. Can you say pre-nup!

Mr. Nerd: Not to be confused with the stereotypical Coke-bottle glasses and greasy hair computer geek Hollywood portrays. This man actually *has* the potential to be a fixer-upper. Though at first glance he may not be an obvious looker, you know he could clean up pretty good with the proper guidance. Mr. Nerd's problem isn't necessarily his looks, its personality. His sense of humor is as dry as the Mohave Desert. His conversations tend to be horridly boring, and often times are sure to send his date running for the door. He tends to talk about subjects that would make most snore…if he isn't stuck in silent mode from his lack of confidence that is. His conversational attempts at impressing her when he talks are what usually kill his quest for love. Unfortunately, it's his inability to recognize it's a date and *not* an I.Q. contest that winds up stranding him at home alone for this season's final episode of Jeopardy.

Ms. Overbearing Mother: The dozen kid pics on her profile page should be a dead give-away, but just in case you're unsure; her profile description should leave *no* question marks. I would never argue, that loving your children and priding yourself on having exceptional parenting skills is more than just a little important. However, she *far* supersedes that stance. The problem with this Ms. is her inability to separate herself from her motherhood role…ever! Her separation anxiety tends to create complications in the intimacy depart-ment more often than not. Oh sure, you may get a few private dates before you're privy to meet her monsters; but future dates will have to be family friendly, as her rug-rats will almost *always* be tagging along.

Mr. and Ms. User: Quite possibly the bottom feeder in the pond of personas, these two are masters of their craft. Of course, I'm referring to them taking advantage. The male version plays Mr. Big, as he proceeds to wine and dine her for the first few weeks. His facade is played *just* long enough to get him in as he figures out what goods she has. The Ms. will make herself appear like she's self-sustaining. She's *all* about independence, until she's earned his trust, then the time is right to start taking. These two have zero conscience as they connive their way into unsuspecting hearts. They prey on the goodness of the "givers" and are arrogant enough to believe, that *somehow*, they deserve everything they get. It's my sugges-tion, the only thing they *really* deserve, is the door…and a boot in the ass to get them through it.

Mr./Ms. High Expectations: Perhaps the saddest of the singles is the "all or nothing" mindset of this Mr. and Ms. They have concocted a list of absolute *must*-haves that will, in the end, be the reason they're still alone. The most confusing part of this persona isn't their desire for what they consider the "ideal," rather the fact that they think they would be worthy of it if it *did* exist. It won't take long to recognize this duo by their incessant need to knit pick what they perceive to be *your* faults. Oddly enough, they are usually *completely* unaware that they have *any* faults of their own. They have a tendency to be obsessive-compulsive. In fact, they can be caught reminding their love interest often, all the ways in which they've disappointed them. Mr. and Ms. High Expectations must have things their way, lest they send you packing—if you haven't already left—that is.

Mr. God Complex: Not to be confused with Mr. High Expectations, Mr. God Complex doesn't believe anyone is perfect...*except* for him. He will always know more than you, be better than you, and his attractiveness *far* outweighs your own. At least, in his "holier than thou" world it does. Don't ever expect an apology when things go wrong. It would be silly for him to apologize for *your* short comings...wouldn't it? He *is* the epitome of arrogance and believes with all that he has to offer...he has the right to be. He is not a un-snagable single, as long as you're willing to bow to this delusional deity and acknowledge his superiority. If you want to leave an impression on this non-God fearing man, be the first one to leave and knock him down a few pegs. He may only be temporarily befuddled, but it's a *great* payback for this pompous ass.

Ms. Vane: She's more than a mere make-over. In fact, she's the *best* butt, boobs and Botox money can buy. You won't find a wrinkle on her face, *even* if it means her eyebrows have to meet her hairline. Her incessant need for nips and tucks, coupled with her constant injections, has pickled her to the point that she's an environmental hazard rather than an option for your next date. However, there *is* a plus-side to this persona. It's almost like you're dating someone new with each procedure, so the chances are, you'll never get bored.

Mr./Ms. Control Freak: It may not seem so bad when this Mr. or Ms. plans your first date. It's nice to have someone else take charge, but it won't be long before they are taking the reins of *all* of your rights. Mr. and Ms. Control Freak have more than a fetish when it comes to finagling their relationships, and their freakish way's kind of border on abuse. From what you should wear to where you should go, it's *their* way or the highway, and *you're* just along for the ride. Perhaps the most bothersome part of this persona is their outbursts, when things don't go their way. It's a less than pleasant experience to be on the receiving end of their anger, and you can be certain you won't want to see it again. In fact, it's precisely these temper tantrums that tangle the weak into their webs. If it wasn't for the fragility of the ones they seek, they'd have *no* hope of having anything that would last long enough to be *called* an actual relationship. Stay far from Mr. and Ms. Control Freak, lest you lose any semblance of a self.

Mr. Meathead: Normally built like a brick shit house, he's *hard* to miss on this list of datables. Though a health-conscious mind would be *thought* to be a good thing, Mr. Meathead takes health to a *whole* new level. One couldn't predict this persona by nights spent in the gym alone, but it would be a dead give-away if his attraction leaned towards "Ms. Airhead." She's the *only* persona that he can hold a conversation with. His other criterion for his perfect potential is that she be a spinner because there's nothing odd about a two-hundred and fifty-pound man searching for a petite one-hundred pound partner. Luckily, you only have to fear coming face-to-face with Mr. Meathead if you fit in both categories, and if you do, you quite possibly could be the ideal match. After all, what could be *more* perfect than being able to bench press his girlfriend?

Ms. Airhead: She's oh so cute and simply put silly, for about the first *five* minutes, then she's oh *so* annoying. You'd have to be bordering brainlessness to tolerate this girls gabbing, which is why Mr. Meathead is her perfect match. Though you may find yourself entranced by her cuteness, try to talk about *anything* past an elementary level, and you're sure to be left *just* as confused as her. She's not the worst woman you could collide with on your journey to finding everlasting love. However, *God* help you if your knowledge of world events is vast, or you like to read. This Ms. will leave your intellect screaming for an escape, and you'll wonder if you had to be conscious in order to have a conversation with her to begin with.

Mr./Ms. Bruised Baggage: These two characters haven't considered leaving their pasts and pressing on to their futures. They have well defined red flag element about them that *shouldn't* be ignored. Your first clue will be their constant need to talk about their ex's. Eventually, you'll find you're the object of their obsession, rather than affection. Watching them sifting through your text messages, or finding them sitting outside your house waiting for you to arrive home—from wherever you dared to go without them—is *all* the proof you'll need. They tend to over-analyze everything you do, in the hopes that in *this* relationship, they'll catch you repeating their ex's hurtful history. They'll deem it necessary behavior, to to ensure that they don't get caught with egg on their face...*again*. You will be forced to explain the smallest of actions, in the greatest of details and even *then* they won't believe you. Unfortunately, this will leave the wrath of all of their misplaced pain and anger pointing in *your* direction. You may try to heal their broken hearts, but you'd be better suited to show them the yellow pages and point out a local therapist—*trust* me—you *aren't* qualified.

Last but not horrifically least

Mr./Ms. Computer Con: If Mr. and Ms. User are the bottom feeders of the dating pond, then Mr. and Ms. Computer Con are the pond scum they feed on. Though a physical description of these unscrupulous individuals is impossible, since they *refuse* to leave the comfort of their computer room, one can only suspect that they are less than suitable to sustain an *actual* in person meeting. They are usually found hiding behind a hacked photo from some poor unsuspecting soul on the net. These individuals build a world of anything *but* reality, as they attempt to suck you into their sick fantasies. It is impossible to know if you're dealing with these duos right out of the gate. However, if you're a month into your computer courtship, and you *still* haven't had a real date...you've been duped.

♂♀

I couldn't *possibly* complete this chapter without the grand finale...Mr. Nice Guy and Ms. Nice Girl. Although I've never actually *met* this elusive, I know he exists, as evidenced by my own father. However, somehow, the word's dad and dating just don't go together...*ewwww*. I saved the nice guy/girl for last, in the hopes that I could end this chapter on a less despairing note, than the chaos that came before them.

I have heard stories about Mr. Nice Guy that usually involved a friend of a friend of a friend. However, finding him has been harder than finding a contact lens...on a glass floor, in a crowded room. I suppose he could be just another urban legend and God "broke the mold"—so to speak—when he made my father. Nevertheless, I will not rest until I meet one, even if he *doesn't* end up with me. So on to the elusive Mr. and Ms. that has become the golden nugget this century. We all know how much gold is worth these days. It's the *only* commodity whose stock has gone up.

♂♀

Mr./Ms. Nice Guy/Girl: Genuine and good hearted are the make-up of *these* gems. Though I could go on and on describing their dispositions, those character traits cover the gamut, and negate the necessity to list honesty, loyalty, integrity and the like. Simply put, they have *no* hidden agendas and tend to wear their hearts on their sleeves. There is no guess work on how they feel about you and they are the greatest givers by nature...that includes communication. These two fit into many life-molds, so there are no specific criteria to get you closer to finding them. There is no "looking for" list to break down where they might be, based on what type of car they drive or job they do. You'll be no closer trying to find out what they might enjoy recreationally or where they may reside. You *cannot* find them by physical features as the physical attributes of these enigmas vary from one Mr. and Ms. to the next. Indeed, their appearance is not the key to finding these mysteries as they come in many different forms. One must get a glimpse of their insides, to know if they've tracked down these treasures. Perhaps one of the reasons they remain *so* elusive, is our own inability to believe that after all of our failed attempts, they're *anything* more than a fairytale. It's hard to see someone when your eyes are closed, and if you've been doing the 21st century dating thing for awhile...your eyes are *definitely* closed. To recognize them, you must be willing to put in a bit of time and *trust* that what you are seeing is real. It should be noted, that while you may cross their path at some point in your search for "happily ever after," you won't be rewarded with this "one of a kind" relationship without possessing some genuine qualities of your own. Many have made the assumption that this persona is a push-over, and though you may get away with it for a *little* while, it won't be for long. Someone with better intentions will come along, and when they do, this duo will desert you. Treat these two like the treasures that they are or lose them and be left wishing you had changed the error of your ways.

♂♀

Perhaps you will be *just* as surprised as *I* was when after re-reading this chapter. I was more than a little taken a back at the bits and pieces of *me* there were, in my list of un-desirables. When I started this journey, I had no idea who I was anymore. I certainly didn't see *myself* as one of these singles. I suppose it's no big surprise that "Mr. Nice Guy" had evaded me over the past three years. Why would I attract what I wasn't willing to give? Then I wondered if I would have even recognized him, *had* I crossed his path? My guess to that question is...probably not. I fully accept responsibility and acknowledge that I didn't deserve him then, but I'm confident in saying I've grown enough to deserve him now. So, I'd like to leave you with a quote that I used one day when I realized what I had been missing, due to *my* own mistakes. Though it is gender specific to me, I'm sure you get the gist.

"Nice guys don't finish last, the women who over-look them do."

Don't waste the space: Make a list of all of the "datable" character traits you've bumped into while online dating...then be thankful they're gone.

Chapter 12

The Singles Syndromes
Defining the reasons we might *still* be alone

"Nothing is more courageous than looking at yourself and admitting, you've got some serious work to do...and nothing is more daunting than actually doing it."

Don't waste the space: Make a list of syndromes your friends have...it will make you feel better about your own.

I f you've been doing the dating thing for a while now, then you're more than likely a little frustrated with your findings. Perhaps it's time to dig a little deeper into the reasons you might *still* be single. There was a distinct point throughout this process, for me, when I started to think that *maybe* it wasn't just them. It took me a while, but I now know that I played a more vital role in my lonely relationship status than I was willing to admit...at least willing to admit to *anyone* else. Harder than deciphering which datable I was dealing with, or even how to navigate the couple creator sites on the net, was to take a *long hard* look at myself. Introspection had become my instructional guide, and the more I dated, the more necessary it became. As if identifying my own singles' persona problems hadn't been work enough *now* I had to sift through my singles' syndromes.

I couldn't see it then, but it eventually became apparent that I was simply *too* busy shopping for my own list of wants while dating. Apparently, I never stopped long enough to think about the things *I* may, or may not have brought to the table. If *I'm* alone, *he's* alone, and *she's* alone, and *none* of us wants to be alone, then *why* are we? In an earlier chapter I made mention of the fact that all these singles I'd spoken with, had the same thing to say. "Nobody takes dating seriously; especially online dating...it's a joke." Even so, how can we say *nobody* when there was a rather large group of us agreeing that dating had become problematic, and that we wanted more? This isn't a representation of just a few people; these were enough people that we could have started our own dating site. I said it before and I'll say it again, it just *wasn't* adding up. How can *all* of these people be single and searching, but *all* still be alone?

Once I took stock of how many dates I had actually been on, I had to ask myself, "Not *one* had any desirable qualities that made him worth keeping?" Maybe they did, or maybe they didn't, I honestly *still* don't know. I'm not suggesting that

I didn't have my fill of freaks while online dating. I'm just wondering how many times it was *me* that fit the freak description.

It was then that my singles' syndromes came to the forefront. The longer I dated, the bigger the syndromes became and the *more* syndromes I came down with. It became *so* bad, in fact, that finding "Mr. Right" seemed farther away than when I started this search. In retrospect, I believe the fact that I was an older singleton and had a lot of baggage in the dating/relationship department was a major factor in my single status. It seemed a likely catalyst in creating things I *didn't* like or *wouldn't* tolerate and that—I'm sure—narrowed the field of my possibilities.

Eventually, there was nothing left to do but try to fix myself and *no* one left to date until I did. Maybe it's just me, but is it possible that *we* are the subconscious creators of our own loneliness?

♂♀

The Seinfeld Syndrome: You don't need to be a fan of the series to understand the seriousness of this syndrome, as the behavior speaks for itself. Someone who suffers from "The Seinfeld Syndrome" doesn't struggle with *finding* dates; they struggle with staying long enough to see past their *own* delusional set of ideals. There's almost always more than one date, before this single decides not to see a person again. The concerns over what they *perceive* to be a physical or behavioral imperfection of their partner tends to take precedence over anything positive. It could be anything from a colic in a bad place to a crooked tooth, or the fact that their partner felt *too* comfortable taking food off of their plate at dinner. One thing is for certain; it is usually something simple, shallow and a *major* misperception of reality. Regardless of their ridiculous analyzes, it becomes an obsession and overrides anything good that *could* be in the works. In fact, this syndrome suffering single can often be heard making statements, like "He/she is perfect, but there is this *one* little thing" and they just can't seem to get past it. "*Little*" being the operative word here, they are either sure to find a *little* something that feels off or fake one. This single can always be found with at least one enabling friend whom they can obsess with, that perpetually gives them a green light to rant about their ridiculous points of view. Often times, that wayward friend encourages them to end what *could* have been a promising potential. If you find that you fit into this phantom problem category, might I suggest you kick your side kick to the curb, instead of your last date? Repeat after me, "There is no such thing as perfection...there is *no* such thing as perfection."

The Butterfly Syndrome: There is nothing like the beauty of a blossoming relationship, which is how this syndrome came on to the dating scene. This single is *so* caught up in those beginning "butterfly" feelings that they start to become addicted to it. The minute something starts to feel comfortable, rather than consuming, they are running for the door. Somehow, they have managed to use giddiness as their guide to gauge whether or not something is good. Unfortunately, they pass on *many* great relationships because of it. Why does feeling settled, start to feel more like we're settling? Isn't the point of a relationship to get to a level of intimacy that *doesn't* require a racing heartbeat *every* time you're together? Perhaps, there are relationships that carry that kind of zsa zsa zsu past the one-month marker, but what happens if you *perpetually* wait for it? My guess is we wind up alone...case in point.

The Greener Pasture Syndrome: The person who suffers from this syndrome *never* thinks his landscaping is as nicely manicured as his neighbors. He/she is stuck in a perpetual state of envy. They are certain, if they could *just* cross over to the other side of that fence, they would find the Garden of Eden. It isn't a lack of luster in their own relationships that makes them ravenous for something more, something different or something better...at least not usually. It's their belief that *everyone* has something they don't, and they want it. The "Greener Pasture Syndrome" isn't a singles' syndrome and relates directly to those that are married or attached. It is, however, many times the singles' lifestyle that lures this sufferer over the fence, which is why they're in this book. Sometimes it's just the monotony of monogamy that seems to get the better of them. Nevertheless, the single is the target of this syndrome suffering non-single. Sadly, if they do take their theory past pretending and actually *cross* the picket fence, the rude awakening that's waiting for them on the other side is a stark reality check that not only *aren't* the pasture's greener, but they can be rather desolate and cause for divorce.

The Independent Syndrome: When you're alone you tend to rely on *yourself*, for day to day things. However, many times that independence can become interfering if you're hoping for a better half. It's good to be able to take care of yourself, and necessary in the singles' world. You just can't become *so* into you, that there isn't room for anyone else. Although the "I'll do it myself" mentality seems minuet, if you're not careful, it can become a precursor for getting *too* comfortable with being alone. These dependents on independence can typically be heard saying things like, "I need some space, you're suffocating me." This single may be searching for "the one," but they usually can't get past the feelings that their personal space has been invaded. Before you know it, their behavior starts to resemble a three-year old that doesn't want to share their toys, rather than someone seriously searching with the hopes of finding their significant other.

~ 100 ~

The Sex Syndrome: This syndrome title says it *all*, and usually develops after a split from a long term union. It stems from the need to build yourself back up again, once things in your last relationship go bad. However, licking your wounds by getting laid *isn't* the best medicine to administer to that broken heart. In fact, this "singles' syndrome" ends up destroying the little bit of self-worth that's left post-division. The only thing you get post-play date is a sense of self-loathing, and it becomes *pretty* hard to get over. By the time this syndrome sufferer realizes their sexapades will not amount to a *real* relationship, the damage has been done. The insecurities they develop from their behavior make them constantly question their interests' intent, especially once they hop off the "sex syndrome" ship...and eventually they will. Intimacy is the loser in *this* game. It becomes a wall of defense, which not only keeps out the game players, but also the good intentions of the *real* deal.

The Cougar/Cub Syndrome: This syndrome blurs the lines of reality when it comes to a lasting relationship. This isn't to suggest that you couldn't be the next Demi, and he might not be the next Ashton. However, Hollywood is a different dimension when it comes to dating...so don't count on it. The reality of the Cougar/Cub syndrome isn't difficult to understand. It's her enjoyment in the ego boost and his lust for the older woman's lessons. Of course, the constant sex *doesn't* suck. The fundamental problem with this scenario is that what starts out as fun many times twists into an irrational fantasy of a future together. While it may be easy to shrug off the stark differences in subtleties like Rihanna versus REO Speedwagon, it becomes much more challenging to reason away his right to have his own children. Often times, she has already turned that page, and *many* others that he hasn't even *begun* to read yet. Eventually, the list of lives must do's become bigger than the love affair, which ends up not only break these singles from their syndrome but usually leaves a broken heart to boot. (Update: Demi and Ashton are getting a divorce ...go figure).

The Beautiful People Syndrome: The single that develops this delusional syndrome is often times a diva or metro-sexual of sorts. However, there is the rare occasion that the average Joe or Joan thinks they are *just* as deserving...and who's to say they're not? The male version can't be bothered with *anything* less than an airbrushed model make-up, and she won't gel with anyone less than G.Q. There are two problems with this syndrome, its lack of sincerity and depth. Unfortunately, looks *can't* buy you love. The shallow structure of this less than satisfying relationship will usually crumble under its well-kept woes. When these singles wake up—and they will—they'll come to the realization that beauty truly *is* only skin deep. Their other "I need a stunner" stance that hinders this syndrome sufferer from happiness is the insecurity they develop by being with somebody that beautiful to begin with. Suddenly, everything becomes more about trust or the *lack* there of. It's a competitive environment, which if you think about it, has very little to do with love. In fact, I would argue they'll only wind up disliking themselves, their significant other or both, if they succumb to this syndrome. He/she must find worth in what lies *beneath* the skin before they can shake this syndrome, and if they do, they often find themselves stuck in the Average Joe/Joan Syndrome, but at least that syndrome works.

The Average Joe/Joan Syndrome: This syndrome forms as the beautiful people jump from their beauty boat, onto to the average single shore. It certainly isn't the *worst* syndrome one could have, as evidenced by the many healthy and happy relationships that form from it. You can spot this syndrome by the beautiful person holding hands with the rather average other. This odd turn of events in this duo's relationship world works, due to the appreciation they have for each other. I'll be it the appreciation is a bit skewed, but somehow they make a perfect couple. One side appreciates how they are idolized for their God given gift of good looks and the other appreciates that their genuine qualities aren't taken for granted. It's the perfect pair really. The competition, mistrust and misuse are gone, allowing the beauties to get their egos stroked, while the beasts get the gorgeous goods. So the next time you see a "Mr. G.Q." holding hands with a "Ms. Average Joan," you won't have to nudge the friend sitting next to you while whispering "Wow what is *he* doing with *her*," you'll know.

The Next Best Thing Syndrome: You don't have to be *too* terribly imaginative to understand this less than subtle syndrome, and you *don't* want to get caught up with one of these needy, non-conscience characters either. Their persona screams "Player" and you'd be the pawn in their game. They are constantly upping the ante at all costs, *including* your heart. To this syndrome sufferer, there's always something more, and they're *not* about to miss it. It isn't perfection that keeps them searching, as evidenced by their throw-away rates alone. The people they throw-away—by any standards—could be deemed pretty damn good in the looks department...so what's their problem? It's the idea that there's something better and it's their goal to concur the "next-best thing." Unfortunately, the only thing this single syndrome *can't* concur is their loneliness. Eventually, they'll be too old to do anything more than ogle what they can *no* longer have.

♂♀

Now that I understood the datable personas, singles' syndromes and my *own* set of singles' diseases that I needed to get over, I was finally ready to find "The One." Well, I was *almost* ready. Disheartening as it may seem, there was more to do...defining 21st century relationships. The idea that there was *more* work to do was dizzying. It seemed too much for a mere date, with no guarantee that I'd ever find that someone special. As I sit here and recollect the long lists of *must* do's and *must* knows in my never-ending, persona-pending, syndrome mending soul search for "Mr. Right"...I'm exhausted. I knew dating was going to be difficult with its new 21st century spin, but it had become almost too difficult.

Suddenly, being alone and happy with *just* "me" was starting to become a serious contender with "Mr. Right." In fact, at this point, my interest in actually *finding* a suitable mate had inadvertently been surpassed by the insatiable need to figure out what in the *hell* was going on with the dating world...and the human race as a whole. My dates were starting to look more like a hypothesis on Darwin's theory than actual dates. I started to use scientific methods to determine just *how* much or how *little* we'd evolved since the decade when boy meets girl was the only precursor to a date.

Chapter 13

FWB/NSA/STR/LTR/The Lifestyle
Defining 21st century relationships

"Don't judge a book by its cover...judge it by its acronym."

Don't waste the space: Make a list of hardcore boundaries for yourself on what you want in a relationship. Refer to this list often...especially when you're lonely!

If you've navigated the net at all, dating sites aside, then you are *very* familiar with the all-powerful acronyms and symbols. We use them in our day to day lives to display our state of emotions. Often times, they are a quick response, when we are too busy to bang it out long hand. In fact, acronyms and symbols have become *so* "in" that we use them not only typing but talking in our daily lives. Apparently, we can't denote a moment out of our busy days, to utter the words "Oh My God." It would seem we only have enough time in a day, to be brief in our exclamation, with their initials "O.M.G."

I don't know if there is an urban dictionary to decipher these important but abrupt announcements, of how we are feeling at *any* given moment. However, when it comes to defining relationships, it is imperative that we understand the point behind the period, of *each* letter used, and the significance of each symbol.

Deciphering the definition of said acronyms, as far as relationships are concerned, is the only way to comprehend the code of conduct for that relationship. Believe me when I say, it *does* make a difference.

Because I was stuck in the mind-set of boy meets girl, boy asks girl out, I just *wasn't* cutting the supposed cutting edge of 21st century dating. There were so many other things at play that I felt like I needed a PhD to figure it all out. Pick the wrong acronym and you could wind up having an NSA with no possibility of an LTR or even an STR...for that matter. This is just my .02, @ teotd if u don't dtr & leave 2 many ??, b4u know it ur left w/o a bf/gf & w/a </3 and that's nothing to lol about. Translation (This is just my two cents, at the end of the day, if you don't define the relationship and leave too many questions, before you know it, you're left without a boyfriend/girlfriend and with a broken heart. And that's nothing to laugh out loud about.)

FWB: You might not know this acronym, but in this day and age I'm sure you recognize the title "Friends with Benefits." However, the question for some may remain, "What exactly does it mean?" FWB should *never* be confused with NSA "No Strings Attached" as they do bear a stark difference. I'm sure that FWB existed *long* before the 21st century, but I'm equally certain that they were fewer and farther between and weren't:

1. Defined as a relationship.

2. As ridiculously acceptable as they are today.

The basic premise of a FWB "relationship" is that you have a friend who on any given night, you could see a movie with, have a drink with or merely stop by for a romp in the sack, if the mood should strike you. It has become *so* popular, in fact, that we've managed to make a movie about it. The fundamental problem with Hollywood's rendition is the ridiculous love story it turns out to be. In reality, it isn't love in the beginning, middle *or* end that fuels this fictitious relationship ...its lust. In the end of this sexual scenario, the only thing that's truly the benefit—if you can call it that—is the friendship should it sustain itself past play time. Somehow, we've misconstrued the meaning of *"friend"* to mean someone I can sexually use as necessary, while I'm between real relationships. FWB really amounts to nothing more than a commitment phobe, who finds a convenient sexual com- panion and labels them a friend. This is simply their attempt at making it more palatable for their playmate of choice...not exactly what *I* would call a friend.

NSA: Much like FWBs, NSAs are just a casual "No Strings Attached" affair, but without the bonus of a buddy. In other words, don't count on a companion to canoodle with, if it *doesn't* include a bed. There will be no wining and dining for this duo and no conversation or cuddling post coital. It's strictly delivering the goods and getting out as quick as possible. While I don't believe the NSA to be the best way to boost someone's self-esteem, at *least* it's honest. A single searching for an NSA doesn't pretend to be anything more than what they *really* are. They admit—some might say honorably—that they are non-committing, nympho-maniacs with a self-centered ego that must be accepted before a stint to the bedroom can ensue. NSAs don't exist past his or her exits the first night, so be certain you want to take that route *before* you have your romp. Many see the NSA individuals as selfish. I suppose, to a degree they are. However, you have to give them kudos for their candor. Although there is the rare occasion this non-relationship slips in an extra evening *if* the goods are...well good. At that point, the best you can hope for is a semi-relationship like an FWB. I have to add, if it *does* move to that status, you still need to realize you are not the only one, but one of some. However, you might get a dinner out of the deal...bonus!

STR: A "Short Term Relationship" is a shoddy deal at best. This sham of a relationship status is based on the idea of time or lack thereof. It can be—in a word—*brutal*. It's a belittling way to go about being with someone. Many times this single touts travel, moving or simply uncertainty on what they might be looking for, as their need for negating a *real* relationship. Quite frankly, most STR singles are hiding behind a pretense of what can be deemed *"somewhat"* of a relationship. However, it's really nothing more than a lie. If someone wants to be with you, they will make use of the time allotted them in life. Sure, travel could perhaps be challenging, but it *doesn't* have to be the breaking point of a relationship. This is nothing more than an excuse and a hidden code for an FWB status. It's a half-hearted attempt at best, to make the relationship *seem* to the receiver, like it's an honest attempt at working towards something serious. If moving was a factor in their fling, why not just call it what it really is...an NSA. As far as not knowing what you want, well *you* aren't worthy to be on the dating scene if you can't figure it out. Quit trying to fool the rest of us with your fake relationship status. I have to add that if you run into one of these less than real relationships, it would behoove you to take a hike. You aren't doing yourself any favors by spending time or expending emotions on someone who is *easily* identified as emotionally unavailable. The shame of this sham *isn't* the relationship itself; it's the lack of this relationship slacker to be honest.

The Lifestyle: The rock bottom in the basic decency of a supposed real relationship, this status leaves a *lot* to be desired...well in the actual commitment category anyway. Desire is the premise of this breakdown in marital or taken promises of "forsaking all others." The Lifestyle is *all* about the masses and the make-believe bond this couple share that allows for others to partake in your partner, with the intent that it's agreed upon. It's an agreement that there will be no backlash for his or her lack of commitment boundaries. "Swingers" is the code for this couple. Simply put, it gives permission to your partner to sexually co-mingle with another couple of their choosing. On occasion, you're given the right to romp solo with another swinger or single of choice, as long as the guidelines, "we're still married" are met. It's a disastrous adventure that has divorce written all over it. If monogamy isn't for you then why get married? Better yet, why bother with *any* relationship at all? You may think you are keeping the sexual spark alive, but there will always be the chance that your partner's playmate might shine *just* a bit brighter. It's a sad excuse to cheat and only builds insecurities. Do us all a favor and stay single!

LTR: If the Nice guy/girl was the golden nugget in the search for the perfect single, then LTRs are the picks in the mountain digging them up. "Long-Term Relationships" seem a thing of the past in this dating dilemma of a century, but on a *rare* occasion, you'll find another that is fascinated by this long ago lasting relationship. Many will tout the want for this "happily ever after" ending only to lure and trap the treasures of the desired datable back to their lying lairs. Whether there's a status depicting their search efforts or not, you'll know *right* away how sincere they are in their search. If their effort to impress you includes a glass of wine and whisking you off to the bedroom, *keep* looking. The LTR individual puts in the proper time getting to know you. He or she is an obvious gentleman or lady of sorts and really understands the concept of courtship. They are goal driven, settled in their lives and have had experiences with LTR's in the past. They are more than happy to share their past relationships with you, but *only* should you inquire. It isn't that the LTR searcher isn't interested in sex. They just have more important items to look for before they get to that part of their must have list, and *more* respect for you than to reap that reward before it's time.

♂♀

It seems pretty dismal when you peruse the list of latest fashions as far as relationship statuses are concerned. The truth is...it *is* dismal. LTRs are yet another rare commodity in 21st century dating, regardless of how many times you see the acronym. However, just like anything else in life that's worth having, it's worthy of your time and effort if finding a *real* relationship is your goal. Sure you will be forced to decipher the difference between a scam and a serious searcher, but if you're going to do the online dating thing, then put on your big girl panties or big boy boxers and *get* to work. If there's one thing I know for certain, it's that I can't be the *only* one wishing I could walk into the sunset with someone special. You have to want it bad enough to do the work, but not *so* much that you'll drive yourself crazy. Trust me when I tell you...it's a *very* fine line.

Chapter 14

To Cliché or Not to Cliché...
That is the question

"If you aren't majoring in philosophy, don't try to be a philosopher....you'll wind up pissing off a lot of people."

Don't waste the space: If you use any relationship clichés...write ten sentences; "I will not use clichés." If someone has used them with you...write ten more sentences; "I will not talk to...."

What is it about a cliché? To the speaker, it seems like a simple and yet profound piece of advice, but to the receiver it feels a lot more like fingernails on a chalkboard? Why is it *so* acceptable for an attached individual to spew their "quoted one too many times" tips on finding "Mr. and Ms. Right?" I'd like to know who *asked* them to begin with. Relationship cliché's always abound when a single starts mingling among the married or taken, and *I* hope to have heard my last one. They are *over*-used, *over*-simplified and I am *over* it. There's nothing poetic about a piece of advice, that really only causes more anguish than it gives hope, when I'm sure, hope was the intent to begin with.

If he or she is, "Out there somewhere," and you *know* this to be a fact, then perhaps you know where I can find him. Stop telling me he's out there "The proof is in the pudding," and you're the spoon for dishing out that advice so "Show me the money." It's a simple thing to say I suppose, but I wouldn't say, such a simple thing to follow through on. This over-simplified attempt at reassurance is only reassuring me that cliché's sound nice in theory, but there's no way I can *actually* put them to practice.

God knows I have met a lot of those *"he's"* and it's still just *"me."* Exactly, how many of them do I have to go through, before "It was meant to be" comes into play? The word "somewhere" only encompasses the vastness of my surroundings and therefore, gives me *less* hope than what I started out with before I was graced with your words of wisdom. Please...*stop*. No *really*...stop.

"It will happen when you least expect it" is yet another painful piece of advice. How can I *not* expect it? I've been searching for a significant other for three years now, and I'm *still* looking. Damn it, I expect it! Is this an attempt to advise me to take a break? Is it a suggestion that the next time I'm renting my—I'm alone on another Friday night—movie at the local Block Buster's, I'll bump into "Mr. Right," while reaching for the newest release? Which is it, take a break or bump into happenstance? I'm going to need a bit more than what is between those lines in order to get this motto. If I'm not expecting it, then *why* am I online dating to begin with? How do you *stop* expecting what you've *been* expecting all along? These cliché's need to die "Somewhere out there" with all the other make believe mantras that are enthusiastically communicated as if they are the antidote to my singles' disease.

My personal favorite is "He'll/she'll come along when the time is right." If that isn't a brain bender then I don't know what is. Who dictates this *"just* right" decision anyway? Is it up to God? Does the universe decide? Is it pre-written that on October 12, 2014 "Mr. Right" will magically appear, and marriage will ultimately ensue? Perhaps it will be the works of the "Great online Oz?" Why should I try at all...*ever?*

If there is a perfect time for the perfect relationship to arrive, I'm completely perplexed as to *when* that could or would be. I feel I have put in more than enough time to satisfy the toughest critic, so what gives? And if time is the precursor to my prenuptial bliss and somehow there's one moment in that time that is just right for it to happen, how long do I have to wait? As far as I know, I only have *so* much time, and then the gig is up.

I can't help but scoff at the ridiculousness of these clichés and would be all too happy to announce that the time to use them has *long* passed. The only thing it's time for is, to give them a proper burial...along with my last bad date.

If I've heard it once, I've heard it a thousand times, "There are plenty of fish in the sea." Surely, that isn't the *best* hopeful advice a person can come up with. Is it supposed to get me through my latest bout of dating depression? I agree there are plenty of fish in the sea...so *now* what? There are also plenty of predators, and *I'm* on the menu most days. Quite frankly, I'm a little tired of swimming in this swamp.

I realize that the cuteness of this cliché is meant to leave me with a sense of easy pickings. However, it's quality not quantity that is the problem with online dating, rendering this cliché obsolete. Personally, I think it should "Swim with the fishes."

Perhaps my *least* favorite cliche of them all is the inevitable, "You're not trying hard enough," which is usually ranted right before "You're trying *too* hard." Apparently, there's a happy medium in both time and effort. If you miss the mark by a minute or a move then it's game over. I think these two cliché's are the cruelest most exhausting of them all. Is this *"just* enough" protocol the same for every instance, on every date, for every day? It puzzles me, I'll tell you. It's the Rubik's cube of online dating, and it *must* be mastered before you can find your mate. The only plus to this game is that there's no timer.

One by one by one, my single sisters were picked off for partnership. "You're next" they always said, but the empathetic stare told a different story. I knew that they didn't believe it—but they wanted to—which is why they said it to begin with. They couldn't bear to be happy in front of me without feeling guilty, so they put *me* next in line to lighten their own burden of bailing on the sisterhood.

Up until those words were uttered, I actually *was* happy for the new couple, but cross the cliché line and my happy tune turned into a sour note. Maybe it was an irrational reaction to a few words, but I reserve the right the reel over this line of bullshit.

Extra encouragement *really* isn't needed. I can assure you most singles have already heard it and don't care to hear it again. The truth is, there's no truth to these cliché's. The *only* time one demands that there is, is when they find someone. Suddenly, it becomes all buttercups and sunshine as they realize the cliché Gods had it right all along when they said, "You'll just know." The truth is, it's a *lot* of work to find someone who fits into your "Love of my life" list and equally difficult to fit into someone else's. There are no magic words to make that happen, but if it does I'm hoping I still have enough clarity to stay away from the cliché bandwagon.

Chapter 15

I Did it for Science

"I never much liked Science and it turns out I still don't...or maybe I just suck at it."

Don't waste the space: Write a positive mantra for your-self...it won't help you find your perfect match, but you won't be as pissed off with a positive attitude.

Throughout my online dating debacles, I had taken every conceivable and customary angle to see that my experience was a fruitful one. Eventually, it was evident that "customary" had become obsolete, due to its lack of producing anything even *remotely* close to a real relationship. It forced me to become more aggressive in my search methods.

I had been a member on every different dating site I could find, which made trying to remember the addresses, login id's and passwords into a part-time job rather than a past time. I recreated my must-have list *so* drastically, that eventually the only thing left was "single male." I reinvented myself so many times over that I didn't even recognize who I was anymore. I was at a complete loss, so I decided to try some unorthodox methods.

You meet a lot of people when you're online dating. However, there was one, in particular, who had become a confidant to me. He gained my trust and made me keenly a-ware, of how I might be perceived by a potential. It came to my attention that I had formed a rather negative aura about me...I can't imagine why. Regardless of what was causing it, apparently it was spilling out onto *every* man in my vicinity. I suppose my optimistic attitude got lost somewhere along the way and according to my new friend; I *needed* to find it again in order to catch myself a keeper. So, I embarked on another journey to remain positive, which included repeating an uplifting mantra every morning.

Every day for three months, I kept myself in a perpetual, uplifted state of mind. Regardless of that crazy road-rager that flipped me off that morning on my way to work or the x-rated email I received from my last login on Match.com, I put a smile on my face. As I tucked myself in at the end of every night, I *knew* this uplifting attitude would make tomorrow a better day. Oh there were days it was difficult, as I got up from the table post date and paid the bill he so casually left on the table. Sometimes, smiling was forced. For instance, while fill- ing out the police report from the man who keyed my car and stalked me for a month...after only *two* dates.

I continued to send up smoke signals of hope, *knowing*, that if I just remained faithful to my newfound optimism, my beacon of light would shine bright enough for "Mr. Right" to see it and come rescue me from the depths of dating hell. Well, that turned out to be *total* bullshit. It wasn't a complete loss though, it was nice not being angry all the time, and I had found a way to better deal with the disappointment online dating had become.

Half point...science.

Perhaps my request was too big to handle all by myself, and it was time to call in the *big* guns. When the suggestion that I send my wish list into the universe was made, I eagerly and happily obliged and sat down to write out my request. Every day I looked at my paper, repeated it out loud and felt empowered by the positive outlook of it all. I answered no profile that didn't have a sign of some sort, *proving* the universe was pointing me in that particular person's direction.

Though at that time I was not a practicing Catholic, it *was* my upbringing, which is why when a seemed to be good Christian man emailed me, I saw it as an opportunity for something different, or quite possibly divine. I was almost convinced I had made the right choice, as I read his email professing his desire to find a good-hearted, spiritual and God fearing woman. I agreed to meet him on Yahoo for a chat, happy that the universe was *finally* listening. It was about five minutes into the conversation, when he began uploading photographs of himself getting out of the shower. I couldn't believe it, but assumed the universe was having a hardy laugh at *my* expense. Then it dawned on me, that perhaps God was just pissed that I had picked the universe over him, so I logg- ed out...and went to church.

Zero points...science.

Thinking better of my decision to diss God and pray to the stars, I got on bended knee to profess my sincere apology. I should have *known* to fall back on my religion. I prayed and *I* prayed, and I *prayed*, until even *I* was sick of listening to what I had to say. I can't be certain when, but there was a distinct moment in time during my prayer vigil, when I suddenly felt insanely stupid and guilty. How could I request such a non-needed thing like a specific single that would fit my selfish needs? I'm fairly sure God had much more pressing issues to attend to, like I don't know...world peace? On the other hand, maybe he was just busy planning the destruction of the the earth over all of the morally lost 21st century singles...just a thought. No matter, I still remained single and his silence was deafening. Then I began to think...maybe the silence *was* my answer.

Zero-points science. Plus one-point...God.

"You have to be more open-minded," I was told. Don't assume that someone has bad intentions *just* from one word or deed. If someone says or does something that makes you uncomfortable or throws up a red flag for you, give them an opportunity to correct themselves. After all, everyone makes mistakes. It's true. We all do make mistakes, and *I* was the perfect example of that statement.

Joseph was a nice man. He seemed respectable after several conversations on the phone. We met for a drink one evening, where he abruptly asked me how I felt about sex. The instinct to run was in *full* force, but I calmed myself and told him politely that I didn't want to discuss it. I explained that although I was no prude, I believed that discussion should be reserved for a later date. Joseph was embarrassed and apologized profusely, asking me if he could make me dinner next weekend to make it up to me. I was quite taken aback. That's *it*? That's *all* there was to it? *Three years* and *all* I had to do was *expect* gentlemanly behavior, and *bingo* there it was?

I gladly accepted his truce offering, and the next weekend met him at his home for a lovely dinner that he prepared. I was sitting in the living room waiting for his return from the kitchen, when I smelled something burning and got up to see if I could help. Just as I turned the corner, I bumped into Joseph buck naked, smoking a bong.

Negative two-points...science.

At the next powwow with the girlfriends, there was a consensus that we had been dating *all* wrong. So many of our taken friends were dating or married to—well—what one would consider a nerd or an "average" man. *Believe* me, I know how arrogant that is, but it wasn't until now that I realized *just* how incredibly shallow I really was. Could one of them be the man of my dreams too? My friends were all happy with their choices; why couldn't *I* be?

I was tired of the arrogance and mistreatment from the hotties I thought I wanted, so I was all about hopping aboard the mediocre mobile and taking it for a spin. In fact, I was looking forward to it. It was like a *whole* other half that I hadn't introduced myself to and the prospects of it all made me smile. I was about to tap into uncharted territory...at least for me.

I sped home, signed on, and emailed Mickey. He had emailed me regularly, even though I had *continuously* blown him off...while in my stupid state. I agreed to meet him for a coffee and the date was rather refreshing. He was quite interesting, polite and intelligent. I could definitely see some possibilities.

We continued to text and email for days after, and we managed to set up the day for our next date. I wasn't over-the-top crazy about him, but there was a different kind of potential I thought I could get used to.

I sent Mickey a text two hours prior to our date to inquire about our destination, as we hadn't made final plans yet. There was no response. About an hour later, I sent him another text *just* in case the first didn't go through...again, no response. In fact, there was never another response again.

Zero-points science. Two-points karma.

I've never been a big fan of science. Perhaps all the "personality tests" I endured while online dating spoiled my speculation, on just how accurate science *really* was. What I do know, is that it hadn't won any extra points through my own experiments. I am of the firm belief, that when it comes to dating, science as a whole should be kicked to the curb for its incredibly obnoxious and inaccurate outcomes. I guess since science is all about theorizing, sometimes your theory is shot in the ass.

With traditional methods out of the window and science sitting at the curb, I had no clue what to try next. It was then that my optimistic attitude hit a brick wall...*again.*

Don't waste the space: Write down your own science projects results...just because I suck at science doesn't mean you have to.

Chapter 16

From Jubilant to Jaded
Shit happens

"Life is like a fast flowing river, sometimes you have to lay back and let the current take you where it may...of course there's always the chance you might drown."

Don't waste the space: Vent, vent, vent...nobody's going to want you if you don't!

U p until this point, I had gotten pretty good at finding my happy face and regaining control over my optimism when it would wane. I was finding, however, that I just wasn't rebounding anymore. I was sick and tired of feeling locked behind my computer screen, exhausted from the less than sincere online relationship shoppers, and plain ole *pissed* off and frustrated. I knew I had tried it all. At one time, I'd of thought it was me, but I had worked diligently to make improvements to myself over the last three years where they were needed, and it changed *nothing* about the outcome. It wasn't just *me* complaining. Every person I came across that had tried or was trying online dating, had the same negative feedback.

I gave up. I couldn't take another cheap chat, not *one* more excruciating email. I no longer had it in me to sign up or sign in, and with the push of twenty "I'm sure" options, I had officially deleted myself from the internet.

I didn't just despise men. I despised people. If there was a way to delete myself from society, I'd of pushed that button too. I hated the men for lying and the ones that were already taken. I hated the women for all of the competition they presented, taking the few good men that *might* have been left. I was pissed at the world. I tried everything from humor to humility and dangerous to demure. It just didn't matter. I restructured my body, broke down my expectations and rebuilt my *entire* belief system, but I was still alone. I was on a self-satisfaction journey now and that would have to be enough.

Now in my second year of college, I had sunk myself deep into my studies, forbidding even a glance at or from the opposite sex. To me, they were a dead species. I had submersed myself in my home life and resided in the fact that I was going to be alone. I stayed out of social settings, stopped talking to my friends and only spoke to my family when I had to. If I was approached at a family gathering that I had to attend, I usurped the conversation and made it about *anything* but my single status. Online dating had been an epic fail for me, and I verbalized that every chance I got, to *anyone* who was single and would listen.

What was so great about a relationship anyway? Why did I want to be beholding to another? Who in their rig- ht mind, wants to sacrifice the things they want or want do, *just* to please another? I didn't *want* to share my space and time. I didn't have enough of it to begin with. It's nice not having to shave my legs for a week or wearing my favorite sweat pants with the hole in the crotch. I *like* that I can scoff down that Big Mac, I had been denying myself of for a year now. I'm *glad* I don't have to worry about exposing my two-week build-up of undone laundry or the fact that I *love* to watch reality TV shows. Who *cares* if my bras need safety pins, and I'm having my period this week? In fact, I'm *grateful* it's over. What was I thinking? Why was I trying so hard to acquire a life that looks now, more like a huge pain in my ass than an end goal?

I was happy being single. Quite frankly, I felt sorry for those that weren't. I didn't want to be a part of those me-chanical make-shift wives and husbands who methodically went through their day. Mow the lawn, wash the laundry, feed the kids and go to bed. I had freed myself from the Stepford syndrome. I was the *real* winner...in the bitterness category maybe.

This "The world can suck it" attitude lasted for quite some time, and I started to wonder if I was the one avoiding friends and family, or if *I* might be the avoided. I just couldn't get past everything I had been through. I couldn't see the goodness in anyone, and I felt the need to return some nasty-ness into the society that sunk me.

Then I found the Italian language. I had always wanted to learn Italian, and I *loved* listening to my great grandmother speak it when I was a child...of course her rendition probably wouldn't be appropriate for a general conversation. My degree required a two-semester course in a foreign language. I was all too eager to pick my heritage from the course list and have a whack at it. Slowly, the culture and sound of the rolling "r" healed my soul. I spoke it as often as I could and plastered it on my Facebook wall whenever possible. I wasn't in love with a man. I was in love with a language...and happy for it.

A friend of mine made the suggestion I put out an ad to find someone to speak this lovely language with, to better my skills. It seemed like a wonderful idea, but I'd have to open my computer to do that, and I hadn't seen *its* screen in months. As I sat down and lifted my dust covered laptop to my login screen, a shard of dating shrapnel pierced my heart. I was angry all over again, but also nervous. Could I be any part of online without getting sucked back into the shameful ways of the www? Would my long-ago addiction rear its ugly head again or was it *really* gone forever?

I logged into Craigslist, clicked on Europe, as I was instructed and with the push of the enter key, ten ads for tutoring popped up *straight* out of Italy. It was the first time I felt excited in a very long time. I clicked on them all and sent a response to each one, hoping that someone would respond...see a pattern here? It wasn't a day, before Marco sent me back an email. We agreed that he would tutor me in Italian, if I helped him with his English. I finally had something to look forward to...and a new chapter was born.

Don't waste the space: Alright, enough bitching, write down something that inspires you besides your want for a significant other...if nothing does, make one up.

Chapter 17

Jerry Springer's got Nothin on Me

"I never said I didn't like merry-go-rounds...I would just like to choose if I want to take the ride."

Don't waste the space: Write down your most bizarre freak-show of a date...then laugh about it because you survived it.

U p to this point, you have read my ranting's, endured my explanations and made it *almost* to the end of my general musings about online dating. However, I would be remiss in excluding this much-anticipated chapter. It's not so much that *I've* been anticipating it—to the contrary—but I've been told by an editor, my English professor, the students in my class and friends, that it *must* be told. Apparently, people will feel jilted if I *don't* air my dirty laundry. Trust me when I tell you that I have acquired enough psychotic stories to fill an entire book. However, I've reserved this chapter for the best bullshitter's and this is rightfully where they belong.

Before I dig deep into my precarious pocket of memories, I'd like to acknowledge that, yes indeed, I was naïve and dare I say...stupid right up until the end. Perhaps gullible is a better choice of words. Nevertheless, I've decided that online dating is kind of like giving birth. Once you've exposed yourself, there's really *nothing* left to be modest about so baring my borderline unbelievable dating history after *everything* else you've read...not such a big deal.

I realize it will be difficult to grasp the concept that anyone could allow such crazy things to happen to themselves or be *that* gullible for that matter. Unfortunately, they *are* my reality from a very unrealistic virtual world. I could write story after story of the deception that is on- line dating, and you'd never get bored. However, there's a special slot for a specific few who aren't likely to be the basic bad story online dating can often times be.

I'm aware that if you've tried this avenue at all, then you've probably been burned by a one-night stand that you told yourself would turn into a relationship. You've had someone show up that turned out *not* to be the person in the pictures. You've probably even had someone not bother to show up or call at *all*. I'm certain you've been lied to about age, weight, marital status, children, goals, interests and the list goes on. These are all basic blunders in 21st century dating, not to be scoffed at, but not even *close* to the chaos I'm about to share.

The following actual stories are in no particular order, with an exception of Marco, because in the end stupid is stupid, it doesn't really matter *what* order it comes in. The names have been changed to protect the identity of the idiots...except for me. If you should read this book, and think there might be a particular story about you. If we went out, it very well could be...or *you* could just be another idiot...period.

♂♀

There's something about Mary: Marcus was a great conversationalist, when it came to Yahoo or emails and with hopeless romanticism as his backdrop, he seemed like a perfect match. Attractive and witty, we never had a pause in paragraphs when speaking to each other online. Our typing went on for hours that turned into weeks. He was often traveling from Michigan to Chicago—my dream destination—that even though I lived next door to, I still hadn't found the time for the trip. I'm not certain why we hadn't spoken on the phone yet, but our most-recent conversation had promised me a phone call. He made it appear as though I wasn't the *only* one that couldn't wait. Although to date, it had all taken place online, the connection was palpable, even without the physical contact. We had the same dreams, goals and ideology on what a relationship should entail.

That evening I declined all other calls, so there were no chances that Verizon would throw him to voicemail without my knowledge, while I was on the other line. I waited up until 3 a.m. before I succumbed to the disappointment that he *wasn't* going to call. I was a bit concerned, but not overly. I knew our connection was solid and surmised that *something* must have come up.

In the morning, I quickly signed into Myspace—which I'm aware now is booty-call heaven—to see if he had left me an email. Clicking through my top friends I realized, Marcus was gone. His profile had been *completely* deleted. I sat befuddled and distraught, as I frantically thumbed through men age 35 in the Shelby Township area for hours, trying to find him again. Did his account get deleted? Was he somehow removed from just *my* page? Did *I* do it? Did Myspace have a major malfunction while I was sleeping for *two* whole hours? For two days, I searched through what was probably hundreds of records, but he was gone. I was devastated, but not as devastated as I was *about* to be.

On the third day, I received an email from an unknown profile. There was no picture and no profile information. In fact, it was the basic format everyone starts out with when they are newbie's. He started with an apology before he got to the meat and potatoes of his intentions for his rather lengthy email.

I was two pages in and past him professing his love for me before he announced he was married. Apparently, they had only been married a few years, and it had been bad from the day they said I do, but he was *still* married. He informed me that he knew what he had done was wrong, but if I could find it in my heart to forgive him, he would be *most* grateful. He went on to tell me that he would be filing for divorce, not that it mattered, but he wanted me to know.

I got to the end of the email and sat for a moment before I responded. I was hurt, confused and certainly wasn't about to date a married man, but I tried to remain hopeful. My return email was filled with forgiveness, and I thanked him for coming clean. I admitted my remaining affection for him and made it clear I *couldn't* date a married man. However, I let him know that if he should actually *get* divorced, I would be interested in seeing him. I even alluded to the fact that I would wait. I hit the send button and waited for what I knew would be his amazement at my composure and his further endearment towards me for my understanding.

The next morning I awoke to yet *another* very long email. I wasn't concerned; in fact, I already knew what it was going to say. "I'm *so* grateful for your forgiveness. You're a wonderful person, and I can't *wait* to be with you." To the contrary, one page down, the mother of *all* deceptions was in just three simple words... "I'm a woman."

Apparently, Marcus was a Mary and although her deceit wasn't intentional it was deceit non-the-less. This woman had been spying on another woman of interest and befriended her as a man to see where her loyalty lied. Unfortunately, I happened to request his—or is that her— friendship in the interim and the rest is history.

Not only was "Mary" bi-sexual, but she was in an open-marriage. This meant *I* was fair game. She apologized profusely. I'll admit that my response was a *bit* odd. I begged her to call me. I couldn't believe it was true, and I *had* to hear her voice. She did indeed call as I cried out of control on the other end while she explained to me that she had fallen in love with me and would like an opportunity to meet me. The mere words left me in the fetal position sucking my thumb for days. I did forgive her, *eventually*, but I'll certainly *never* forget.

I don't know what concerned me more about this chaos. Perhaps it was the fact that I was talking to a woman the whole time or *maybe* it was the knock on my door from her husband three days later. He had brought me cookies and flowers to solidify the sincerity of their apology...Google be *damned*!

Jack and the Big Apple: New York, what could be more appealing to an aspiring writer? He was handsome and...well handsome. His intellect bared a close resemblance to Sylvester Stallone in Rocky I, but what he lacked in mentality he made up for in muscles. He was adorable and easy to talk to, which incidentally we talked on the phone every day. He was America's finest Italian descendent, and it was looking more and more like he could be mine. We had a lot in common, *including* bad marriages. His wife had left him with two very young boys for another man and a life of drugs; he hadn't seen her in two years.

Jack made it a point to profess his love to me every day as he went into great detail about how wonderful it would be if I lived there with him. It wasn't long before he had me convinced to cam, but to my disappointment his wasn't working. Oh he *did* turn it on, but all that was visible were horizontal lines of color with a hint of movement on the other end ...nifty little trick I've since learned. He promised to get a new one by the end of the week, which made me anxious and he knew it, so he tried to settle my worry. Within an hour, he called and put his son on the phone to say hello. I mean what could be more reassuring than being known to the children. "You'll be meeting Karen soon" he told him, sucking me deeper into his sadistic fantasy.

The next day while I was pushing for a new cam, he announced his mother had taken ill and was in the hospital. He ended the call rather abruptly telling me he would make contact, as soon as he could. My heart hurt for him. I knew how close knit his family was from our past conversations. It helped calm my nerves when his sister logged into Yahoo and left me a message to let me know how things were going. Two days later, silence had gotten the better of me as I left concerned messages on Yahoo, *every* hour on the hour. We seemed to be playing tag. He was never on when I was and one of us was *always* leaving a message for the other.

I was completely heartbroken when I received the message that his mother had passed, and he would be on a flight to Italy where she would be buried in a family plot. I left a heartfelt "I'm terribly sorry" message and let him know

I was there for him when he returned. Immediately, I ran to the store and purchased a sympathy card, looked up the address he left me on Yahoo and sent it *right* away so he would receive it when he returned home.

A week later, I received an email stating his wife had returned, and they decided to work it out. I was *dumbfounded*. To add insult to injury, I received the sympathy card—I so carefully picked out to soothe his aching heart—that same day stamped...no known address, return to sender. I was hurt but honestly mostly just embarrassed that it happened *again*. Why is the absurdity always *so* much more obvious in retrospect?

Save a horse ride a cowboy: Normally living in New Jersey, Joseph was currently in Oklahoma, caring for his sick father's ranch. We were initially just internet friends, sharing the ups and downs of any given day. Many times, I would unload on Joseph, giving him brief but thorough descriptions of my previous mishaps with online dating. He was *all* too empathetic and was keenly aware of my guardedness.

A man with a Native American heritage, our conversations were intriguing, and I enjoyed learning about his culture. Raised on an Indian Reservation, he had so many thought-provoking insights on the soul and life as a whole. He was not a well-to-do man and was barely making ends-meat, which was something I understood *all* too well, being a single mother.

White Cloud was a nearby chief that had befriended Joseph's father years before and who was making regular house-calls to rekindle Joseph's upbringing; as well as helping Joseph's father prepare for his impending last journey home...to heaven that is. I was touched by Joseph's stories about his dreams. He always shared them in great detail, and they *often* included me. Little by little, we grew closer, and I began to let my guard down.

I never questioned Joseph about *why* he didn't call me. I already knew that his town was far from his home, and he didn't like to leave his father. Joseph received his groceries and the like from White Cloud when the chief would come for his weekly visits.

When Joseph wasn't caring for his dad, he was working on the Ranch, which left him little time to do anything else. He did promise me he would buy some minutes and invest in a cam, but he couldn't be certain when that would be, so I continued to wait...patiently.

Night after night I sat typing on Yahoo, and even though I had done this before, he seemed *too* sincere, *to* faith filled of a man to deceive another. Besides, how heartless would someone have to be? He knew my past; he wouldn't *purposefully* betray and if he was one of those, my sob stories would certainly find his humanity and deter him from continuing.

From time to time, my past naiveté would come back to haunt me, and I would question him about his intentions. However, my insecurities never lasted long. Joseph didn't bother with excuses; he would just apologize for his situation, and somehow it made it right and our friendship continued.

One night, about two months into our online affair, he signed in and told me White Cloud was on his way. His father was in transition. He asked me to stay with him online, and of course, I did...for *six* hours. I walked through each step of his Native American tradition of passing as it was happening, and I felt a sincere compassion for Joseph. I was touched that he wanted me there. I was, for all intents and purposes *with* him during his father's passing.

Christmas was only a week away and then came New Year. It was about 11:00 p.m. my time when my phone rang. It was Joseph. He called to wish me a Happy New Year. I was quite taken aback. You would *think* from the shock of his call, but it was the sound of his voice that confused me. He sounded rough, older and *very* unlike the 28-year-old man I had been typing to for months now. I brushed off my instinct to question him and thanked him for his call.

It was about a week later when I had written a blog about deceit on the internet. I honestly don't know *why* I wrote it, I suppose my feelings that night brought up skeletons from my un-emptied dating closet. Joseph was a regular reader of my blog, and his comments were frequent, so I wasn't surprised to see one following my latest post. It was the content of his comment that shook me awake. "This blog is about *me* isn't it?" I knew right then and there that *once* again my instincts were right, and I had been wronged yet again.

We spoke only briefly via Yahoo that night, when he confessed he was 50+ years old, *didn't* own a Ranch and his father *hadn't* passed away. There was *no* White Cloud, *no* rituals and *no* Reservation. I promptly deleted him and ig-nored his plea for forgiveness. I had been in the forgiveness business *too* much these days, and I just didn't have it in me.

Two years had passed and Joseph sent me an email on Facebook. It was then that I finally forgave him for his fakery. Although I will *never* understand the source of these outlandish stories in an effort to stalk the sincere online, I figured it made me a better person to forgive him. It must have bothered him, or he wouldn't have looked for me to begin with, and *maybe* it taught him a valuable lesson. I'm hoping the niceties and forgiveness of one helped him bury his Native American bullshit story along with White Cloud *and* his non-existent dead father.

The West is gettin too wild: Texas was a nice state, and Tom was a nice man. We met on Hot or Not, which wasn't *exactly* a dating site, but still an opportunity to meet people. Please make a note that this was *very* early on in my expedi-tions. I had already had the experience of being burned when it came to anything online, so I was readily prepared for any red flags. After a week of Yahoo and email chats, we decided to speak on the phone, which encouraged me—I'm sure part of his master plan— to feel more at ease with his intentions. He spoke in great length about a very bad experience he had while online dating that *truly* put my horror stories to shame. It was another comfort measure to be certain he cinched the cynical out of me while he slowly and methodically laid the foundation for his filthy plan.

We had made the decision after a month to meet up in Chicago for New Year, right under the Christmas tree by the ice-skating rink in the center of the city...what could be more romantic? Of course, I *wasn't* going to go alone, but I had three months to find a friend to tag along. We had "phone" dates every Friday where we took turns picking a movie of our choice and meticulously timed when to start the video, so we were watching the same scenes. It was the next-best thing to an actual movie date and although a bit tricky, *great* when it worked. It was our unique way of spending quality time together since we couldn't be with each other in person and the romanticism of it all didn't hurt either.

We had been dating online style for about two months when the inevitable issue of distance was discussed. Tom was finishing up his degree at a local college while he worked for their athletic department, which incidentally I *did* do a background check on. It would be another year before he was finished, but he proclaimed he would have no issues moving here to Michigan if things continued to go well.

A year sure seemed lengthy to wait, *especially* without the needed human contact and the opportunity to see if we gelled in person. We decided we would take turns traveling back and forth to build on the relationship we had started.

As the date for our romantic meeting loomed closer, Tom started questioning me in weird ways. "Are you open minded?" It was starting to make me uncomfortable, and I wasn't certain where he was heading with his line of questioning. I had already seen him on cam. I talked to him on the phone and spent hours discussing different aspects of our lives...he *seemed* normal.

It was when he initiated a three-way phone call with a male friend, and they began reminiscing about a time they spent together, *not* in the "Hey bro, it's good to see you" kind of way that I realized *I* was the odd woman out.

I'm still uncertain if his odd phone call was meant to make me run, or if I was merely an innocent participant in his rainbow parade. Either way, the *only* thing Chicago was going to see that New Years was a lot of snow ...minus me in it. Honestly, I'm not sure what the bigger disappointment was, that there had been *another* assassination attempt on my optimism or the fact that I wasn't going to Chicago.

Italy gave me the boot: As mentioned in the previous chapter, Marco and I had agreed that we would help each other with our native languages. I had *really* fallen in love with the Italian language, *so* much so that my professor requested I accompany a small group of students in the Spring to Italy for a study abroad program. I felt rejuvenated. For the first time in a very long time, I had something to look forward to. I wanted to make sure what I *did* know was impeccably spoken, so having Marco in my life at that time was paramount.

The time difference was easily mastered since he worked a night shift and could get online while he was working. We would spend hours on cam as he taught me the language of love, and I taught him the language of...well English. A sincere friendship had formed over the next month. We shared stories about our lives and day to day excitements as well as disappointments. He started to become an essential element to my days, and I relied on him to make the bad days better and the good days the best.

It was shortly after that he introduced me to Skype. I eagerly set it up on my phone and waited for his call. It was *amazing* to hear his voice, and we talked for an hour. Three times a week, he would call me just to say hello, but I think he called because he enjoyed making fun of my American accent as I desperately tried to sound Italian. He made me laugh and that was something I had *really* needed to introduce into my life again.

It was at the end of one of our chats on Yahoo that he uttered the words "Ti Amo." (I love you). I had been developing feelings for him, but knew *all* too well how it would end; just like *every* other long-distance relationship had in the past, and this was some *serious* distance. However, I chose not to hold back as I uttered the words back "Ti amo mio caro." (I love you my dear). Our friendship relationship went full steam ahead from that moment forward, developing into a made for TV love story.

Marco had worked in the states a few years back and was willing to move here—they're *always* willing to move here—but the hopeless romantic in me was eyeing ways I could make the move. I had visions of grandeur as I saw myself writing books by a window that overlooked a beautiful vineyard. Could I *really* have found the love of all love's in another country? If I had why, why, *why* did it have to be so far away?

We started to talk every day. He even introduced me to his daughter via cam as our relationship continued to blossom. He would always describe his trips to Palermo to visit his parents on the weekends and send me photographs of their walks around the town. If it wasn't for my children, I'd of hopped a plane in a heartbeat. I was scheduled to travel to Italy in May for school, which was eight months away. We often daydreamed together about our walks through the streets of Rome, stopping for Gelato. He was a *master* at creating daydreams. It wasn't a week later when he announced that he couldn't wait that long, and he was planning a trip in the first week of January to come visit me. He had some vacation time coming up and his mother would watch his daughter while he was away. I was *so* incredibly excited. I could hardly contain myself.

From time to time, I would question him on his agenda as the date drew closer. "Did you look for an airline ticket yet?" He always reassured me that it would be no problem for him to catch a flight out of Rome and *even* went as far as to give me a list of flights he had been looking at. Of course, I checked in to those flights the *moment* he gave them to me. I wasn't about to be burned again. Any mild complaint or hint of mistrust was quickly extinguished with an adequate remedy or solution. Marco was great when it came to making me feel comfortable.

It was a few weeks out, and I was actively putting together a Christmas gift to send to Italy. It wasn't anything expensive, just little trinkets for him to have that would remind him of me when we couldn't talk. I was a bit taken aback when he gave me his work address to send the gift to. I tried not to be cynical as he explained to me the horrendous postal conditions in Italy. "I'll be sure to get it if you send it here," he told me. Sensing my withdrawal he started to give me his home address, but I stopped him. At *some* point, you have to trust or move on. I did Google the whole "poor postal service" idea, and that rang true so I paid my fifty dollars to send him his gift and I felt really good about it. *So* good in fact that I checked with him every day to see if he had gotten it yet.

It was only two weeks before his scheduled arrival. I was sitting on the edge of my seat. This was it. He was either the *real* deal or I was being scammed yet again and the only way to know for sure was if he showed.

The closer the date got the less he talked about it and the *more* disheartened I became. I was at work one afternoon when he pinged me. Marco had me upload the "Ping" application to my phone over a month ago so that we could text each other for free. It was another attempt to get me to calm my nerves about his intentions, since he was at my beckon call. He was just inquiring about my day, and I'm sure ill-prepared for my breakdown, but I had been working myself up for three days to get the courage to ask him about his impending travel plans. "You aren't coming are you?" I was *baffled* at his response. It was as if he never made mention of it and had *no* idea what I was referring to.

I was absolutely beside myself and unable to hide my frustration, disappointment and disbelief, which apparently made him unable to keep me as a contact. He deleted me *completely* out of his life. He disconnected me from any avenue of contact, and I never spoke to or heard from him again. I did send him an email. I wasn't expecting a return email and really I didn't want one. I don't even know if he received it, but it was *my* attempt at closure. I needed closure from him and from online anything. I said to him *all* the things I wanted to say to *all* the others that went before him, but never had the opportunity or the wherewithal. It wasn't a written lashing by any stretch of the imagination, rather a heartfelt letter, requesting he gives some thought into his deceptive ways and the lives it can potentially destroy.

The real disappointment was the gift that had finally arrived two days later. When I received the notification via email I cried from frustration, and then I laughed. At least, *something* turned out to be true in the end...Italy's postal service sucked!

♂♀

I don't think any of these men hurt me because they were no longer in my life, in fact, I don't think any of these men really hurt me at all. In reality, *I* was the puppeteer in my own daydream play. I wanted to have faith in the human race and in doing so, often times believed to a fault. I *wanted* to be loved, to be *in* love and was willing to travel over oceans to find it. The saddest turn of events wasn't the deception; it was the desperation I felt and obviously displayed. It made me an easy target. The fact that I was willing to mistrust myself and my intuition in order to see my happy ending come to fruition was the *worst* deception of all. It was an expensive lesson; one that cost me *many* membership fees and my personal dignity, which in the end, is *too* much to gamble with for the game of love.

Chapter 18

And So It Is Written...
And so it is done

"It can be frightening when your path is uncertain, crowded with tall grasses and what lurks before you is unknown. Then I think how boring it would be if the path was cleared and you saw everything that was ahead of you. It's the bad on the path that strengthens your character and the good that makes the unknown path worth traveling to begin with."

Don't waste the space: Write down what you've learned from your experiences with online dating...if you haven't learned anything yet go back to Chapter One.

In the end, my journey *was* a fruitful one. Though I didn't find what I *thought* I was looking for—love—I found something worth *so* much more...myself. As I look back over the chapters and reflect on all of my experiences, I realized that each one was a necessary stepping stones to get me to where I am. Furthermore, where I am, is where I *need* to be, if I should ever find "The One." In fact, had I not taken this journey I wouldn't have recognized "The One" if he had shown up. Of course, I'm pretty sure before I finished this process; I probably wouldn't have been very appealing to him anyway. My "AD" days were initially an embarrassment to look back on, but they were a developing factor in the woman I've become. Building profiles was an opportunity for me to decide who I was as I filled in each like or dislike and tried to leave an image of the person I was, in written format.

Rebuilding my profile wasn't really reinventing myself, it was evidence of growth in the woman I was evolving into, ridding myself of the unnecessary and learning my *true* must have list. The datables and syndromes were guidelines for what I *didn't* want and what I *needed* to overcome. All the chapters that followed and were in-between were *my* baby steps to becoming whole again. I regret nothing and I'll remember it all. Even my most horrific, yet memorable dating debacles will have a place in my heart. Without them, I may not have recognized that naiveté, even gullible and *yes* sometimes stupid were and are my make-up. I'm okay with that though, it means I have hope. Hope in myself, in my future and hope in humanity to give it another try. We are so inclined to use those words in a negative tone, but without those character traits, I'd of given up *long* ago.

I made friends along the way, ones that I will be *eternally* grateful for. Their guidance and grace were the elements that held me together when the world let me down. They were the evidence that goodness *still* existed. I learned a lot from people that started out strangers, and even though we may never cross paths again, they *profoundly* changed the way I viewed my circumstances, my possibilities and myself.

It's *vital* that we realize our boundaries. Without them, we are vulnerable to the most vicious attacks, those that come from within. People can't hurt you, if you know what you will and will not tolerate, and you stay true to yourself. Knowing who you are and what you want, what you need and what you'll allow are precursors to *all* possibilities in life, not just love. The moment we bend in order to fit into someone else's idea of what we *should* be or blur the boundaries of reality and the 21ˢᵗ century's virtual world, we become our own betrayers, and *we* are the only ones to blame. Online dating is merely an avenue to meet someone you wouldn't ordinarily have an opportunity to meet. *Yes*, there are a *lot* of non-sincere searchers, deceptive datables and unwanted whack jobs. However, there are also many others that are looking with honest intent. The only way to find them is to find you first.

Get rid of the must-have lists. In the end, you will realize that finding a partner who loves the movies or jogging everyday as much as you do *isn't* so important after-all. Sometimes, it's the differences not the similarities that you bring to the date that are the *most* valuable and intriguing. You have to learn to love yourself, your life and what you have *without* a "somebody" before you can be completely prepared for anybody. Finding the perfect person is the sweet filling, *not* the whole cake.

I spent ample time complaining about dating sites, requesting something be done about the setup. I learned to hate technology and believed it to be our demise. The truth is it isn't technology that has failed me; it's the users of the technology, *including* me. I was given the opportunity; it was up to *me* how I seized it and what I did with it once I had it.

There will always be those that take advantage and those who are taken advantage of, but if we can learn lessons from these experiences, then our experiences can no longer be considered mistakes and we will be richer for it. Although love may *not* conquer all and online dating leaves a lot to be desired, I *still* think it's worth the journey. With a hint of hope, a pinch of perseverance and a dash of deciphering who you are; you are certain to build a recipe for something quite spectacular if you can only wait for it to rise.

Don't waste the space: Write down your new hopes and dreams for your perfect match along with a new must-have list...compare it to your first ones for an eye-opener, much shorter isn't it?

Chapter 19

P.S.
And then there was Michael

"Sometimes when one door closes, it opens the whole world...not just a window."

Don't waste the space: Write down a list of people's names who you think should buy the book and send them to Amazon.com or Kindle...my job here is done.

Armed with my new knowledge and the new enlightened me, I eventually *did* log back in. It wasn't long before I had received my first email, and it turned out to be the first one in more than *one* respect. I was hesitant to open it, uncertain if I could start this all over again. I knew I was sporting a better attitude, but I *still* didn't know if there would be something that would make me snap or hurt me...and I was in no hurry to repeat past mistakes. I was actually surprised I received an email at *all*. I had left my profile fairly blank, just a picture and a few incidentals. It occurred to me that I would be less of a target if I *didn't* write my life story and every detail about my life's passions on my page. However, I was pleasantly surprised by this particular email content. "How are you today?" That was it; that was *all* it said. It was one small, but very sincere sentence. It didn't move mountains or make me sink to my knees, but it was normal and normal was *exactly* what I was hoping for.

We met for coffee at a local bookstore a week later, after we had several comfortable conversations on the phone. Michael made it known right from the get-go that he wasn't big on emails and preferred only a few phone calls before we met in person, to see if we clicked. It was a refreshing change from my past.

His smile was *all* I needed to know that he was *indeed* something special. I had found a "Mr. Nice Guy" and quite possibly *my* "Mr. Right." Our conversation was filled with laughter, and our coffee quickly turned into a dinner invitation—the same night—*unheard* of! It was the first time I ever had a hard time leaving after a date and his request for a kiss goodnight, only endeared him to me more. He was respectful, intelligent, fun and intriguing; I couldn't *wait* to see what would happen next.

Our second date found us with notebooks, so we could make a couple's bucket list that entailed anything and everything, from a trip to Chicago to a walk in the park. This level of comfort was foreign to me, not just from the online dating scene, but from any and all relationships I had before I even met Michael...*including* my fifteen year marriage.

It wasn't long and our second date had turned into a third and then a forth, followed by a fifth and a sixth. Without even realizing it, we were checking things off of our bucket list and adding others. I *even* managed to make it to Chicago, with Mike by my side of course.

It was *easy*, effortless really. Eventually, I stopped waiting for the proverbial shoe to drop and started to look for the sunset. Suddenly, it seemed I had *too* much space for just me, and I couldn't seem to get *enough* time with him. Without warning, my feelings changed and mowing lawns and doing dishes seemed like a wonderful past time...as long as we were doing it together.

It was in September 2011, when he took my hand and asked me to marry him and on June 23, 2012, I will *finally* see that sunset I've been searching for, as I walk down the isle with *my* "Mr. Right." I can only say thank you while I give a proper plug to "Plentyoffish.com" for giving me the opportunity to meet this wonderful man.

So, as I place the last period on this page, and I end the last paragraph of my peculiar journey, I leave you with this thought.

"Happily ever after *will* happen...when you least expect it."—Hey, I said I would *try* not to get on the bandwagon—*try* being the operative word.

The End